View from the Rear of the Lion Rock, Cheddar.

MEMORIES OF CHEDDAR

Chris Howell

BIBLIOGRAPHY

Atthill, Robin	*Old Mendip* (1964)
Atthill, Robin	*Mendip: A New Study* (1976)
Camden, William	*Britannia* (1586)
Balch, H.E.	*Cheddar, Its Gorge and Caves* (1935)
Compton, Theodore	*A Mendip Valley* (1893)
Coombs, H. & Bax, A.N.	*Journal of a Somerset Rector* (1930)
Coysh, A.W.	*The Mendips* (1964)
Gough, J.W.	*The Mines of Mendip* (1967)
Hopkins, Mary Alden	*Hannah More and Her Circle* (1947)
Horne, E.	*Idylls of Mendip* (1922)
Howett, William	*Rural Life In England* (1838)
Irwin, David & Knibbs, A.J.	*Mendip Underground* (1977)
Johnson, Peter	*The History of Mendip Caving* (1967)
Knight, F.A.	*The Heart Of Mendip* (1915)
Martin, E.W.	*Country Life in England* (1966)
Pavey, Rowland	*Water-Finding and the Sublimated Faculty* (1909)
Pickford, Bernard	*The Mendips: A Geological Study* (1976)
Pritchard, Lewis	*The Story of a Mendip Lad* (1975)
Seeley, Edith	*Under Cheddar Cliffs* (1903)
Shipham, Sarah	*Notebook and Diaries (1842-1872)*
Wyrall, Everard	*The Somerset Light Infantry — 1914-1919* (1927)

By the same author	*Some of Our Old Pictures* (1979)
	Round Here, in Them Days (1980)
	I Have Heard Tell . . . (1982)

First published in Great Britain in 1984 by
Chris Howell, Chapel Cottage, Chilcompton, Nr. Bath.

ISBN 0 947660 00 3

Printed in Great Britain by Purnell and Sons (Book Production) Ltd., Paulton, Bristol.

ACKNOWLEDGEMENTS

My role in the making of this book has been that of middle-man. The pictures are not mine and nor are the stories; I have merely sought them out and pieced them together in what, I hope, is an attractive manner. It was Douglas Gough who suggested that it should be written. He had seen other books that I have done and felt that I should produce a similar volume about Cheddar. My sincere thanks to Doug for his kind thought then, and for his great help since — and to Dorothy as well, for looking after the garden while Doug was helping me (!).

Besides Doug and Dorothy there are dozens of others who have helped me in various ways. Their names are recorded below with, in most cases, an indication of their involvement; the italic numerals refer to pictures and the others to the stories. I tried very hard to use only local pictures but in a few cases this was impossible and so the ones on pages 34, 62, 63, 94, 97, 99 and 122 are 'foreigners'. Also, the young man seen on page 82 is really Percy Channon and not George Hale, and the lad in the picture on page 46 is a Cheddar boy and not Ivan Chard who is telling the story about his Uncle Charlie from Midsomer Norton.

I mention in my introduction the kindness that I have been shown in Cheddar and without the generous help of the following people the book would not have been written. Therefore, my very genuine appreciation goes to:

David Adnett; Harold Athay (42, 45, 53, 77b, 98); Robin Atthill (*110*); Paul Barnard; Walt Binning (43-44, 79-84, 97); Birgitta — who puts up with far more than there is space to mention; Mrs Bishop (*117*); Chris Brice (*90*); Miss C. Brice & Mrs M. Craddock (90-91, 92a, *93*); David Bromwich of the Somerset County Library, Taunton; Martyn Brown of the Museum of Somerset Rural Life, Glastonbury (*94*); Ivan Chard (46, 87-89); Roger Coombes; Arthur Coombs (77a); John Cornwell; John Cottle; Mr F. Cox (108); Mrs F. Crump (92b, 93); Jim Curtis; Jean Edwards; Jane Evans of the Woodspring Museum, Weston-super-Mare, (*9, 10, 11, 30, 33, 52, 114*, and endpapers); Mrs E. Fountain (104-106, 109); Mrs F. Fountain; Jack Gait (107); June Gilberthorpe (*72, 73*); Ann Goodwin; Doug Gough (*13, 18, 21, 22, 24, 25, 26, 27, 37, 47, 55, 59, 65, 78, 100* 9-26, 72-73, 124b); Enid Gough; Jilly Harris; Margery Hicks — Aunt Marge (*48, 49, 51,* 27, 49-52, 70-71, 74, 76, 103); Bob Hill (30-36); Jim Hill (112, 121-126); Melvin and Di Hill, who were outstandingly kind with their time and help (*cover, 32, 38, 39, 40, 42, 50, 54, 56, 61, 64, 66, 68, 69, 70, 71, 76, 77, 82, 84, 85, 86, 87, 108, 123, 124, 126*); Melvin's mum and dad; Dave Irwin; Colin Jay; John, for being John; Reg Jones (38-41); Ernest Lane; (*116*, 113-118); Lis — who is still a world record; Mary Mare (*103*); Adrian Moon (*53*); Richard Maggs; Richard Moon; Jack Moss (57-58); A.N. Other — so modest! (43, 94-96); Bill Parsons for much vital help (*14, 20, 45, 54, 60, 67, 74, 79, 80, 89, 91, 98, 101, 102, 104, 105, 106, 112, 119, 120*); David Parsons; Bob Patten; De Pickford; Lewis Pritchard (110a, 111); Tom Randall (*12, 16, 17, 19*); Hazel Rider (!); John Sanders; Mrs G. Say (*109*); John Scourse (29, 75, 99-102); Richard Shearn (*97*); Annette Smith; Rex Thomas (*43, 46, 113*); M.J. Tozer; Dr Sadie Ward of the Museum of English Rural Life at Reading University (*31, 34, 62, 63, 99, 122*); Wells Museum; Weston Library (*36*); Weston Murcury — for extracts from articles by Francis Brooks (60-69); Mrs Nina White (*57*); Marion Wickham; John Wood; and, finally, my very special friend Austin Wookey (54, 56, 110b).

PREFACE

Having finished the book I now have to write a foreword; but what to write? Well, what I have tried to do is to put together a collection of pictures and anecdotes about Cheddar as it once was. When you visit the place today you will find it teeming with tourists from all over the world; but, what is now a torrent, began hundreds of years ago as a trickle. Many of the early visitors were drawn from my side of the Mendips, fifteen or so miles away, and I am by no means the first from this neck of the woods to write about the attractions of Cheddar.

A regular visitor and commentator at the beginning of the last century was John Skinner, the Rector of Camerton. He would often risk foul weather and foot-pads to get there, sometimes travelling alone and on horse-back, in need of 'some change of scene to change my ideas'. On other occasions he would bring guests to see the famous Cheddar Cliffs, but, despite his thrilling to their spectacle, he would almost invariably record his irritation at the 'craving peasants and dames' who pestered him to buy their polished stones and flowers. Having seen the Gorge and haggled with the 'aged matrons', he would then pay others to guide him and his friends into the cavern, which they would view by candlelight. Then, 'the regular routine of clambering, chattering and cheating having been performed, and the horses put to their carriages, we proceeded on our route . . .'

A hundred years after Skinner did his journeying, Dom Ethelbert Horne of Downside Abbey went for a bike-ride. In order to reach Cheddar, which was his destination, the good Ethelbert had first to weave his way between the myriads of rabbits which in those days spread themselves so innocently across and along the Mendip roads. When he had successfully negotiated the rabbits and avoided the donkeys and geese that roamed freely on Priddy Green, Ethelbert soon reached the top of the Gorge and was then able to free-wheel the last couple of miles into Cheddar. He had come that day to visit 'a patriarch of Mendip', the Magdelanian caveman whose bones had been discovered a few years earlier. His guide in the cave was 'an uncouth boy who has learned by heart all that he has to say by way of information, and he screams it on a single high note, forgetting that we are but two, and not a party.'

Now it seems to me quite possible that the boy in question was young Douglas Gough, whose grandad found the caves. But Horne calls him uncouth. Doug Gough is a lot of things, but uncouth he ain't! I first met him early last year when he called on me to suggest that I wrote a book about Cheddar as it was when he was a lad, seventy years ago. His yarns and his photographs — and his flattery! — were too good to ignore and so I began my own series of trips over the Mendips.

From the very first day of working on the book I have been overwhelmed by the kindness and encouragement I have been shown by the people of Cheddar, and compiling the material has been an enormous pleasure for me. I hope that Doug is pleased with it, too, because it is for him and Dorothy — Lady Gough! — and for all their friends, and mine, in Cheddar.

Chris Howell

Chilcompton,
Somerset.

February, 1984

"We found more than two thousand people in the parish almost all very poor; no gentry, a dozen wealthy farmers, hard, brutal and ignorant. We went to every house in the place and found every house a scene of the greatest ignorance and vice. We saw but one Bible in all the parish and that was used to prop up a flower pot . . ."

"There is as much knowledge of Christ in the interior of Africa as there is to be met with in this wretched, miserable place."

Hannah More, 1789

"Of course, there have always been caves here in Cheddar, but not like the ones the tourists visit. Once upon a time they were homes for cavemen and wild animals; bears and lions and such-like. And people were still living in them for many years after this drawing was done. Cheddar used to be very different to what it is now. Going back eight or nine hundred years, a chap called Henry of Huntingdon reckoned that Cheddar was one of the four great wonders of England. He wrote about a Cheddar Hole which was *'a cavity under the earth, which though many have entered and there traversed great spaces of land and rivers, they could yet never come to the end.'* There's nothing like that here today, and no-body is certain what it was or where it was. Any amount of money has been spent since,

looking for it. A lot of people say it was the Gorge itself but others think the entrance must have been blocked up by rock falls and the muck and waste washed down from the lead-mine workings on the Mendips. That, and when the road was built down through the Gorge in the 1790s.

Although there's no Great Hole to be seen, visitors have been coming to Cheddar for centuries to see the Cliffs and the original caves. There were always poor people, living in the caves and cottages in the Gorge, only too pleased to make a few pennies by showing them round by candlelight. There was a Rev. Skinner who talked about a dozen or more so-called 'craving peasants' pestering him for his custom in the 1820s. Then, in 1837, George Cox — Grandfather's uncle — discovered the first of the modern caves.

And he discovered them by accident. Old George was a corn miller who kept some tea gardens. The story goes that he needed somewhere to put his waggons so he started to build a carriage-house. Well, he sent a fellow across to the hillside to fetch some stones and after a bit he began to realise that the chap was a long time gone; so he went over and found him in a gaping hole in the ground, yelling, *'Help! Get me out! I'm in hell!'* What he'd done was fall through into one of the chambers. And that's how Cox's Cave was found. And that was the start of it all.

Then Grandfather came to Cheddar. He was Richard Cox Gough, whose mother was George Cox's sister, so his interest in caves probably stemmed from his childhood when he'd visited his uncle's caves. By the time he arrived he had already done more than most men do in a

lifetime; he'd been a sailor engaged in the ivory trade off the West Coast of Africa, then he became the captain of a sailing ship going backwards and forwards to the West Indies. When he left the sea he retired to Bristol where his family were millers. He'd been left a wholesale tea business — the Congou Tea Warehouse on Redcliffe Hill — but he knew nothing about tea and managed to lose a considerable amount of money. After that bit of misfortune he became a school teacher, would you believe it, and after that a permanent-way inspector on the Bristol to Exeter line, before it amalgamated with the Great Western. Somebody said he did everything by turns and nothing long. Then, in the middle of the 1860s he came here. I know that he still had an aunt here then, Sarah Shipham. She'd married a whole series of Wesleyan Ministers; four of them, including a missionary When she died she left nineteen guineas to the Trustees of

Cheddar Wesleyan Chapel to be used for their worn-out Wesleyan Ministers and Widows Fund. And well she might! She'd worn out enough of them herself!

When Grandfather arrived here with his wife and family they lived in a cottage in the Gorge opposite an old couple called Jack and Nancy Beauchamp, who were apparently living in a chamber in the cliff face, eking out a living by showing visitors the inside of their cave. To make his own living Grandfather worked up at the lead mines on the Mendips, walking up and down for two shillings a day. They had very little money at that time, couldn't afford joints of meat, so they kept goats from which they had their milk and butter and cheese. William King, who had the lime kilns next to their cottage, built an oven in the side of them for Grandma to cook her goat-meat for the weekends. It's still there today. And that's how they lived. Pretty basic.

There was a cave, a hole in the rock, up by the reservoir in the Gorge, and, to supplement his miserable income, Grandfather used to show people around with a candle, for a couple of pence. Then, when he'd been in Cheddar for some time, he started to go over and chat with Jack and Nancy, trying to persuade them to move out, so's he could see what he could find in there. There was a tumbledown building right against the rockface — whether t'was a pigsty or a cottage goodness only knows, but he said, *"If I can get that built up for you, will you move out of here and let me in to see what I can do?"* Anyway, after a bit the three of them formed some sort of a partnership and the couple moved out. And Grandfather started his work.

Like everyone else, Grandfather knew of the story of the Cheddar Hole and he would have dearly loved to have been the one to rediscover it and so, once inside Jack and Nancy's cave, he began to excavate. I've got a copy of a letter that Father wrote about Grandfather's first cave. Here, read it:

'The caves discovered by my father, the late Richard Cox Gough, in 1877, are not now on view, and it is doubtful if they ever will be, as the new caves he discovered on the same premises about 80 yards away, in 1898, far surpass anything discovered in Cheddar up to date. My object in writing is to take a walk through the 1877 cave which I have always thought very wonderful — so did thousands of visitors. Well, to begin with, the entrance is a long arched slitter. The first chamber is not very lofty but the rock formations are wonderful. There was a short tunnel on the left so Dad thought there must be another chamber in that direction so he began building some very deep steps of boulders — some of the steps are quite two feet deep; there are about thirty of them. There was a small opening at the top sloping upwards, which meant a bit of climbing; after crawling through Dad found it led to a vast chamber. There was a drop of about fifteen feet and at the bottom there was a deep pool of water.

It was impossible to take visitors into the cave that way, so he drove a tunnel at the top of the steps, through solid rock, to let the water out. He had about twenty men working by night, carrying out clay and stones down the steps in buckets. The work was hard but well worth doing. The chamber was not only wonderful, but beautiful. It is ninety feet high, with quite a lot of stalagmite formations.'

Oh, that was a huge chamber — a terrific place, and with all the stone he'd blasted out he built a great stone pillar and lit it up with acetylene gas. Then he put a light on top and told people they could see the moon through a hole in the roof. The only time I went in there was with my cousin, donkey's years afterwards. We shone a torch up to see the pillar and there was a crash like a clap of thunder. What had happened was, we'd disturbed all the bats hanging there — thousands of them — they came from all over the place. Caw, we got out of there pretty smartish. Frightened me silly. I never went back in there again.

'I forgot to mention . . . you ascend a very fine stalagmite floor which leads to another passage which was cut through solid rock and stalagmite until Dad came to another very beautiful little chamber called the

Queen's Jewel Chamber. Not content with this he went plodding on, cutting and blasting his way through. Finally he burst through to another very beautiful chamber, the Cathedral Chamber — as the other one, small, but full of sparkling beauty.

I think, now, I have told you all I can remember regarding the old cave which was once on show, but I am often plodding up and down the steps in my dreams. At the time of the discovery in 1877 I was only about six years of age, but before I was twelve I was able to conduct parties through the caves as well as the next.'

We all did that. When I was a lad the guides were paid £2 a week, but they did well on their tips. They got some fantastic ones. As youngsters they used to ask us to go round with them. We were supposed to be there to watch that folk didn't touch things — break things off for souvenirs. Then, as we were getting towards the exit the guides would give us a couple of pennies and send us on ahead. The visitors didn't know but what we were tourists like themselves and as they were about to leave we'd give the money back to the guides. *"Thank you very much, Sonny,"* they'd say and rattle these coins in their hands. They'd soon start piling up the tips. Then, perhaps, they might give us tuppence for some chocolate for helping them with their tricks.

All the time Grandfather was searching for new things to improve his cave system. With his sons and his helpers he must have removed hundreds of thousands of tons of rubble and deposit from the caves. His first breakthrough was in 1893 when he found the Fonts and then the Swiss Village, and five years after that he made his greatest discovery; he finally broke through into St Paul's Chamber and then into King Solomon's Temple. The instant they'd found them, Grandfather sent a workman out of the cave to fetch the rest of the family, and when they'd come he gave thanks to his maker and they all sang 'Praise God from whom all blessings flow'. Between them they'd discovered the fantastic caves folk visit today.

From then on it was open competition between the Coxes and the Goughs to attract the visitors to their caves. The Coxes had placards and posters saying that Edward VIIth had

visited their cave so the Goughs countered that by printing a brochure that said: *"Don't be deceived re. King's visit to Cheddar. Edward VII commanded Lord Knollys to write and say he was quite young when he visited Cheddar. Fifty years ago! Never been to Cheddar since!"* But they seem to have missed one good bit of advertising: in Sarah Shipham's diary she's got a bit from a local newspaper printed in 1852, *"Large parties have lately visited the cliffs, gardens and cavern. Among other distinguished guests who have honoured this neighbourhood with their company we find the following entry in the visitors' book under date of 12th inst. 'President Fillmore and Party. United States America.'"* I've also got a pamphlet which the Goughs used to distribute down at the station, which says, *"Visitors are warned to beware of touts outside Cox's cave. They are said to be an intolerable nuisance. Don't be molested but*

go straight to Gough's." That picture is of Grandfather with one of his Cox cousins. Privately they got on all right, but when it came to business they were up to all the tricks in the book.

You see he's got his pipe in his mouth. He kept a different pipe for every day of the year. He had his private smoking house built up on a ledge in the Gorge and had a heap of rifles up there in racks all round the walls. He used all the pipes he had — meerschaums, silver mounted ones, all sorts. Father was the same, he'd keep one going in his mouth, one in his pocket cooling off and another one all ready charged up. The same when he went to bed even, he'd light up when he was between the sheets and have another spare one filled on the bedside table.

Grandfather was always passionately fond of animals. He had birds, dogs, monkeys — all sorts. Used to take his monkey to church on his shoulder — the vicar never minded. Tame jackdaws he had, and they'd talk. He's got a couple of them there, look. He'd split their tongues with a silver sixpence and have them talking. You ever heard that done? He'd do that and then teach them words, so Father told me. And did I tell you about his donkey? Well, he had this beast which had carried all the muck and stones out of the caves in panniers, and then, to his dismay, just before he was ready to open, the donkey died. He was heartbroken. All the time while they'd been getting the caves ready, he'd been setting up a little museum with all the bones of mammoths,

and cavemen, and tools and coins — it all went in there, and he reckoned that this little donkey had earned his place. So he set to and skinned it. He cleaned the skull and put that in a case and then pegged up the skin to dry on a rock, behind the museum.

The very first week that they were open they had two old lady visitors, who were so proud that the man who had discovered the caves was showing them round in person. They wanted to know the ins and outs of everything — a bit of a nuisance, really. When they finally got back to the mouth of the cave there were five people ready and waiting to go in — at a shilling a time, mind, and no-one there to attend to them. Grandfather got very agitated, 'cause after their long struggle they were desperate for money. Anyway, these two old dears were still pestering away at him, wanting to know everything about everything, when they arrived at the skull of the donkey. *"What's that, Mr Gough? What's that?"* By this time he was losing his patience. *"Ladies,"* he said. *"That is the jawbones of my ass. And if you'd care to come round the corner, I'd be pleased to show you the skin of my ass." "Oh!"* they cried. *"You horrible old man!"* And off they stormed. But he was exasperated and just couldn't resist it.

Grandfather may have been a showman, but he was a very religious man, too — a very moral man — would never normally swear or say a word out of place. His rudeness to the old ladies was really because of his money worries. My father had even gone to South America when he was 21 to make some money to help. One of his brothers had already emigrated. They were a family of ten, mind, and with all the expense of excavating and one thing or another, Grandfather could do with every penny he could get. So Father sent cash home. Then, when he'd saved up quite a bit, he came back with quite a large cheque from this South American bank — in Chile I think it was — to be cashed in London. Well, it took weeks to travel in those days, and by the time he got home the bank had crashed. I've still got the cheque. While he was still out there he had a card from Grandfather, *"Had a marvellous week. Taken £5."* Caw, they'd take that in five seconds now.

Four years later Grandfather was dead. But what he had achieved! So much. And then his sons took over and carried on his work. On one occasion they were making a drain and they thought they'd try to divert the water along a passage-way and down into the underground river. After a bit they found a stalagmite in the way — sort of covering the floor — so they got a

GOUGH'S NEW CAVE DISCOVERED
NOV 12TH 1898
ELECTRICALLY ILLUMINATED
TWO OR MORE PERSONS 1/- EACH
GOUGH'S
ILLUMINATED

crowbar and a sledgehammer and started working away at it until suddenly the crowbar went through a skull. And there was a skeleton, with the bones laid around him as if he had died standing up and the body had just collapsed. It turned out to be a prehistoric man — between 40 and 80,000 years old, they reckoned. That was in 1903. Then, two or three years later, with the advent of the motor car and the charabanc and whatnot, they felt they ought to have a car park. All round the entrance was solid rock, but behind where the present restaurant stands there was a slitter going up, all filled with soil. The bank came right down to the ground and they decided to dig into all the earth and scrub and level it out to make the parking space. Well, one day when they were doing this they dug in so far and a damn great lump of stone came sliding down and immediately they found a stone coffin, complete with skeleton and pottery and jewellery and things. Then soon after, they found another skull with more coins. Roman, it all turned out to be.

Around to the right there was the first chamber that Grandfather had worked on, and one day we were hanging onto the ivy on the rock-face and shuffling along a narrow ledge to reach it when, lo and behold, we found another cave with coins and bones and engravings. Oh, that was an exciting time to be growing up in Cheddar. And some grandfather for me to have, eh? The biggest regret of my life is that he died two years before I was born, but I've always felt very close to him — he still means a lot to me. Would you tell people how proud I am to be his grandson?"

"Oh, Mr Gough was a lovely old gentleman. I remember when he found the cave in 1898 — great excitement here there was. And I was one of the first ones to go in — a great treat. It was a shilling then but we went in for nothing 'cause we were local. And if we wanted to we could take friends in free — didn't matter how many there were as long as the one with them was local. Old Mr Gough would never open the caves on a Sunday though, unless it was for overseas visitors and then he wouldn't charge them. They'd have to pay him what they thought was right and he'd give it to the poor old people who lived in the Gorge. About fifty years ago there was a concert of the Cheddar Carols that the BBC broadcast from inside the caves. If you want to know about Cheddar you really ought to know about the Cheddar Carols."

Smoothly.
Key A♭.
1. When right-eous Jo-seph wed-ded was, Un-to a vir-tuous
maid. A glo-rious an-gel came from heav'n, A glo-rious an-gel
came from heav'n And to this dam-sel said.

2. "Hail, blessed Mary, full of grace
The Lord remain with Thee.
Thou shalt conceive and bear a son
Our Saviour for to be."

3. "It's wondrous strange," said Mary then
"I should thus blessed be.
How gracious is the Lord to men.
To all the world and me."

4. Then spake the angel Gabriel,
"Tis not the work of man
It is the work of our great Lord
E'er since the world began."

"Well there were six Cheddar Carols altogether, all handed down from generation to generation by word of mouth. Then in 1899, when Fred Scourse, my father, was the church organist, he got an old chap called Tom Gilling to sit in the corner and Father wrote them all down while the old boy sang them. Father had sung them himself as a boy but I imagine old Tom was more authentic, being of another generation. When my sister was a senior lecturer at London University, she delved into old carols and found a very obscure one from Southern Ireland that had a strong similarity to one of ours. So perhaps one of the Irish beggars who used to travel around over here brought it over with him centuries ago. I don't think they're ever sung anywhere outside Cheddar. I've never heard of it happening elsewhere."

"From about 1700 onwards, the Anglican Church treated Cheddar very badly, because, like so many other parishes in the country at that time, there were absentee clergymen. High-born families would arrange for the living of Cheddar and such places, and one man might hold several. They might be in Yorkshire or Leicestershire or somewhere, and all held by some chap who was at Oxford or Cambridge or off on the Grand Tour. This character would draw £400 for the living and then appoint a curate at £20 a year, and that wretched fellow would live into old age hoping for a church of his own, with an income. The result was that Cheddar had a succession of boozy curates who had long since given up — just did it for the money. There was one whose only contact with the place was to ride over from Wells to take a Sunday afternoon service. People were being buried without a service and children were not baptised. The Church was just disintegrating.

And then Hannah More came on the scene, determined to do something in the way of spiritual improvement, as well as social and educational advancement. Hannah was a highly intelligent lady who lived with her sisters at Cowslip Green. She was born in 1745, when her father was a headmaster in Bristol, and she had gone on to write and, indeed, had a play successfully produced at Covent Garden. She also had some highly influential friends, including people like Garrick, Wesley, Dr Johnson and Sir Joshua Reynolds; and it was really because of one of her close chums, the slave abolitionist William Wilberforce, that she became so involved with the well-being of Cheddar and the surrounds. He had been staying with her at the cottage and she sent him down to see the sights of the place, but, instead, he returned to Cowslip Green deeply affected and distressed

by the deprivation and depravity that he had witnessed. He shut himself away in his room for a few hours and then came out and announced, quite simply, that something had to be done and that if Hannah would undertake the work, he would foot the bill.

The first thing Hannah did was to open a Sunday School. In 1789 she took a seven year lease on a cottage and appointed a teacher, a Mrs Baber, who lived in one end of the building, with the children being taught at the other, in what had been an old ox-barn. There were 140 children registered to begin with, and from that start sprang a dozen or more schools in the villages around Cheddar. Children were encouraged to work by means of rewards. They'd get a penny if they attended four weeks running and another if they could recite parts of the Bible.

Sometimes they would be given gingerbread to eat, and once a year, shirts and shoes and aprons and suchlike were handed out to children with good records. Such was the poverty in the area that those were prizes well worth working for. And then, having seen the children cared for, Hannah turned her attention to their parents. For the most part they couldn't read or write or sew and so she organised day classes and adult evening classes for their improvement.

Like most other communities, Cheddar had its men's friendly society. These chaps clubbed together to look after their own interests, paying in a couple of coppers or so every week and then drawing on their funds in the event of illness or injury. Once a year they would have a great social gathering and it was of such importance that if any man failed to turn up, or was improperly dressed, he would be fined. The annual club day was a proud event in the

calendar of any village and all the members would parade in their best bib and tucker, and carrying their staves — and invariably ending up with a feast and excessive alcoholic celebrations.

Hannah More decided that the ladies should have their own society, albeit a more refined one; a club for the social improvement of those who joined. It was called the Cheddar Female Society and the members paid in three ha'pence a week with the subsequent benefits; three and six-pence a week if they were ill, a pair of white woollen stockings — knitted by Hannah and her sisters — together with five shillings and a Bible when they got married, seven shillings for a confinement and a guinea when they left this world. It was all done to perk up the morals of the neighbourhood, I suppose. And woe betide any lady who succumbed to bad language, or drunkeness, or — dare I say it — whoring, 'cause she'd be booted out, pronto, once and for all.

Hannah and her helpers started friendly societies in other villages as well, and if she thought things were bad here in Cheddar, she really had her eyes opened when she went to Shipham. It was a mining community and she reckoned that it was one of the most wretched villages on Mendip; *"the people savage and depraved almost beyond Cheddar, brutal in their natures, and ferocious in their manners. They began by suspecting we should make our fortunes by selling their children as slaves. No constable would venture to arrest a Shipham man lest he should be concealed in one of their pits and never heard of more. No uncommon case!"*

Of course, Shipham was an important centre for the mining of calamine, which is used with copper in the manufacture of brass. They discovered it here, on the edge of Mendip, in the middle of the 16th century and, as a result, Bristol became the centre of the brass business in England, if not the whole of Europe. I understand that Hannah became so disgusted at the price the poor miners were getting for the calamine that she did something that would be unheard of today; she built a shed and bought the calamine from these chaps at a reasonable price, and so cornered the market. In that way the brass founders had to buy the stuff from her at a decent price, and she made sure that the chaps who dug the stuff got the money.

Incidentally, there is an interesting link between the village clubs in Somerset and the local brass industry. Pretty well all the clubs in the county, and twenty or so elsewhere, had very distinctive, fashioned brass heads for their staves. Each club had its own emblem — a crown or a spear or an acorn, perhaps; that sort of thing. Beautiful, some of them. Cheddar's was a turned knob affair. It really is something peculiar to Somerset, and I daresay that if they hadn't found calamine and made brass hereabouts then we shouldn't have had them either.

Another thing about Hannah; there wasn't much in the way of reading matter for the likes of the simple Cheddar folk, and what there was wouldn't have appealed to Miss More very much, and so she and her helpers took to writing tracts for distribution to these people and their like elsewhere. And so successful was she, that within a year she had sold two million copies.

Once a year Hannah had a great get-together for all the children from the villages in which she had done her good works. The first one of these was organised within a couple of years of her starting work in Cheddar. Callow Hill was a focal point between Axbridge, Shipham, Rowberrow and Cheddar and on that first occasion she took more than 500 children and 300 adults up there. She had half a dozen clergymen to help her and between them they fed the whole enormous gang with beef and bread and cakes and plum pudding, all of which was washed down with cider. After that, Hannah's Mendip Feast became an annual affair. It was a day out and a half! Parents and children would pile into carts and go up there with their grub and sit at the top and have games and races and general merrymaking — a real bunfight! And probably prayers. Hannah More was a great character and no mistake."

Cheddar Village & Cliffs. W5618.

"We went down tuh Cheddar 'bout 1910, fer the choir outin', along wie the vicar. That were the first day's outin' that I ever 'ad, an' we wen' in Mr Morgan's two-horse brake. There were a dozen on us — eight, nine an' ten year olds. Course, we 'adn't never bin tuh Cheddar afore, an' nor 'adn't the vicar. He come to Mids'mer Narton from Australia, so 'e certainly 'adn'.

Well, we wen' past Priddy an' as we got down into the Gorge we did see these cliffs gradu'lly gettin' higher an' higher an' we wondered where in the Hell we were goyn' — what were happenin', see? Half way down Mr Morgan said, *"We'll stop the horses now fer a bit, an' let 'em have some grass, let 'em 'ave a feed, 'cause there ain't no more down the bottom. The kids can play round here, Vicar, but don' 'ee let 'em climb up on the rocks there, 'cause thass loose stone."*

Well, I soon managed tuh get away from the rest an' vound a crevice wie plants in — ferns, an' things like that — an' that were just up my street. An' then it 'appened! I caught a liddle frog. A very, very tiny frog. I zed, "Whass be us gonna do wie he, then?" Well, we 'ad a crate o' ginger beer up in the brake, those bottles wie the glass marble in the top what you did have to press down. I thought, "I knaw what we'll do wie'n." An' I got one o' they bottles an' mixed in some water an' then I got that liddle frog down the neck an' past thik marble. Well, then all the ginger come to the top an' there were this liddle creature floatin' round in the middle an' we didn' know how we were gonna get'n out. So we put the bottle back in the crate an' shut up. Then off we went, wie the vicar an' there were this liddle creature floatin' round in the middle an' all on us sittin' back in the brake an' the horses joggin'

down nice an' quiet, wie the brake on. We 'ad food wie us an' while we were eatin' that, one on 'em reached down an' picked the ginger beer bottle up. Uh zed, "Look Vicar! Look whass in 'ere!" An' the vicar zed, *"Le'ss 'ave the truth now. Oo've bin playin these games? 'Cause 'e waddn' put in there down Mr Prior's ginger beer factory. Come on!"* So I zed, "I'm afraid I'm the guilty one." *"Aha,"* uh zed. *"I thought Jonesey 'ould be in it. I thought he'd be responsible. Now, 'ow be us gonna get'n out?"* 'Same way as us got'n in there I reckon, Vicar. We'll float'n out.' I pressed down the stopper an' empt out a bit o' the stuff an' gradu'lly got'n tuh crawl out. *"I feel happier now,"* zed the vicar. *"I shouldn'a 'ave liked tuh 'ave thought he'd a bin stuck in there."* Oh, I 'ad some time wie that vicar — but 'e thought the world of I.

When we got down intuh the bottom there weredn't many people about. T'was clean there then; a nice place to be. Some on 'em wanned to go in the caves an' some didn'. I always reckoned t'were a burnin' shame that the caves were owned by people. They should belong to everybody. It's natural, see. A cleavage in the rock. Stalagmites an' stalactites all hung down gleamin' an' glistenin'. Beautiful. Anyway, I didn' bother tuh go in. I wanned tuh go roun' all the nooks an' crannies an' find out all the odds an' ends. After a bit, me an' my mate what I 'ad along wie me decided tuh go up Jacob's Ladder. He waddn' very strong an' I ad' tuh practic'lly carry 'e up the top; I were a biggish young 'un, mind. Well, when we'd a bin up there for a while t'were time tuh come down agen, an' I never bin suh frightened in me life. I weredn' frightened when I started down the coalpit a couple o' year later, but I were too frightened tuh come down thik ladder agen. I looked down an' thought, "How in the hell did I get up here?" Anyhow, eventually two or dree chaps seen us an' come for us.

So we got back down. Some on 'em 'ad bin in the caves and some 'ad bin in the gardens. Everybody 'ad a tale to tell. Then the vicar ast 'ow long it 'ould take tuh get tuh Weston. *"Oh,"* zed Mr Morgan. *"That'll take us another 'our wie the 'orses."* That were about tea-time already, but we went tuh Weston, s'nuh. We got down there an we saw the sea. Oh ah, we saw the sea, an' the tide were comin' in. I 'ad'n never seed the sea, s'nuh, an' I never thought it'd look like that.

We 'adda good time down there, never 'ad no money though; coul'sn't buy anythin'. But Vicar did shell out a few coppers fer a few sweets an' then he treated us all on the donkeys. We 'ad a nice afternoon. But then we 'adda go 'ome. By the time we got back at night they 'orses 'ad bin 32 er 35 mile an' t'were comin' up ten a'clack an' our mothers an' fathers were sweatin', an' the vicar 'ad tuh take each on us home tuh make things look good.

Next day I were tellin' me father all about it an' he zed, *"Well,"* uh zed. *"Thou's seed the sea as many times as I've seed the sea. Thass once."* That were one o' the best days I ever 'ad. I 'ahnt know whether the frog enjoyed it or no, but it didn' kill'n, see. I should'a brought'n back home wie me. You know, that day is one of the things that duh stand out in my mind. That were beautiful."

"That landslip was in 1906. After that there was a big outcry and the quarrying had to stop. My eldest brother always worked up there till then, and he often used to tell us that before the slide they would stick a bar up against the rocks when they finished for the day, and many times it would be pushed over when they went up next morning; so it was always moving little by little. I suppose the workings must have weakened it too much and it slipped. Every Monday after school I had to scrabble up there with some dinner for him, but when we got out that particular day I went up with Johnny Scorse and Fred Williams. We were stood in the road by Gough's caves when Bill Mutter came up the road with his steam waggon and we ran out and caught hold the back till we got to the weighbridge. After we'd seen what we wanted to see we went on home. A lot of the great boulders are still there, just where they fell."

"Oh, good heavens above! Old Betsy Card, what used to sell the spar — fancy stones — up the Gorge. How ever many years ago was that taken? Now, you've seen one of these here ladies on a broomstick, haven't you? Well, she were the spittin' image of one o' they. She were hook-nosed, knock-kneed and spraw-footed."

"Now, thass a load o' rubbish, what he said about Betsy. Years ago ev'rybody was a witch to some people. In those days, if anything was going wrong in Cheddar, the people would say they were 'haggerided' — thass what they did call it. Get salt and throw it over their shoulders 'cause they reckoned someone was haggeridin' 'em. An' the salt were s'posed to stop it.

A hundred or so years ago nigh on everybody believed in witchcraft. If any old lady was a bit different to the rest, folk 'ould reckon she were a witch. They said the old women could stop people in their tracks as they walked along a road an' keep 'em there, frozen to the spot, fer as long as they felt like it. They reckoned that witches could only get into yer house if they come down the chimney so they'd shove pins an' needles an' things into an animal's heart an' stick the blessed thing up the chimney so's she'd stab herself on the way down. An' they were s'posed to be able to take on the shape of cats or dogs or whatever. There was a time when anything that went wrong was blamed on these poor old women; if someone took ill and died, if cows gave no milk or hens laid no eggs, then some old biddy would be responsible. They really did believe it. Did you know that once upon a time there used to be a Wise Woman and a Wizard living in Wells and folk from round here used to travel for miles to get their help?

No, Betsy and the others weren't witches or anything of the sort, they were just old women who scratched a livin' by sellin' things to visitors outside their cottages in the Gorge. All of them've bin pulled down now, but you can still find garden flowers growin' up there where they used to be. Betsy's cottage came down when they built the car park up there but it was fit to fall down anyway. It were what were called a 'Night House' or a 'Key House'. If folk could build a house for themselves overnight, and have a pot on the boil by daybreak, they could claim the house an' ground fer their own. What they used to do was build 'em roughly with whatever material they could lay their hands on, like rock or turf or bracken, an' then, when they'd made their claim, they could set about makin' a proper job of the place in their own good time. Most of them were built in the roadsides like Betsy's were up the Gorge.

Two or three of these women lived up there when I was a boy. When there'd bin blastin' up at the quarry they'd go up an' pick up the pretty stones an' polish them an' shine them to show the beautiful milky colours. Then they'd sell them from their baskets. Other times they'd climb up on the rocks to fetch ferns an' Cheddar Pinks to sell. Cheddar Pinks is a flower that do grow up in the cliffs, it's got a lovely smell, but it won't grow in a garden, just in the rocks. Mrs Brooks an' Ann Thatcher used to sell these things as well, but not as much as Betsy Card. *"Oh, my stones are better than your stones."* You know the attitude."

"Now, I'll tell you a story about Betsy Card, no lies. I was going up the Gorge one night and she was standing in the doorway with her arms out on the doorposts, *"Come on in,"* she said. *"Come on in."* Well, I went the ten or twelve steps up her garden path and there was a great big pig in her garden. I went inside and it was a little place with a curtain across with her bed behind, and there was a table and chair and a fire-place with more smoke goin' out through the door than up the chimney. It was a very humble place she had. Anyway, in the room there were eight or nine little pigs, about a month old! They'd all gone under her bed so I took a stick and rattled it about a bit till they came out. Turned out that this pig had wandered four or five miles down from a farm on the Mendips and settled down in Betsy's cottage. That's the truth. Oh, I remember Betsy Card ever so well."

"When I were elebn I useda take parties down there twice a week wie me uncle. Two waggonettes — six or eight in each. Folk ud get up parties an' we'd pick 'em up 'an leave Mids'm'r Narton at eight in the marnin'. I didn' really have tuh drive, my horse ud follow Uncle Charles's in front — all's I had tuh do were put on the brakes goin' down the Gorge. We put the horses behind the Cliff Hotel, but we had tuh watch out 'cause they from Weston ud steal your harness or your chaff. There were some devils about mind. After we'd fed an' watered 'em we might take a wander up the caves an' go in fer nothin' 'cause we'd brought a party down. A lot on 'em useda have a strawberry tea but we alus took sandwiches. A heap on 'em went down there just tuh get fruit fer jam makin', 'cause did pay tuh make jam in them days, s'nuh. After we'd done wie Cheddar we'd harness up agen an' go back through Wells. About 1912, that were. Cost 'em half a crown each."

CLIFF HOTEL
HOTEL
BAR

"That big picture was the Queen's Jubilee in 1897. Mr Franklyn, who kept the Cliff Hotel in those days, was a very jovial man. Mother always tried to dress us in pairs, two alike you know, and she'd deck me and my next sister in blue dresses. When Mr Franklyn saw us he started singing, *"Two little girls in blue"*. Oh, I can hear him now in my mind's eye. He thought t'was lovely. When Father died we were dressed in black. Absolutely black. My mother was very religious minded and she brought us up very strict. Though I was only seven I had to wear dead black at first. I was the youngest of 13, ten survived and one of my older sisters made the dresses and that, and little silky black hats to go with them. After so many months we were put into half mourning so that's why we were in these little black and white dresses. Nobody on earth had a mother like we did. Beautiful she kept us, but mind you she worked. I can honestly say that we never wore our Sunday shoes to school. They were cleaned on Monday mornings and I can see them now, all put along the shelf ready for the next Sunday. And there weren't many in those days who had two pairs of shoes. Mother had nothing when Father died, no pension, no nothin', and she had to take in washing and I stayed home to help her. That's where we lived, behind the tree there, with the wash house on the side. She had a big copper in there with tin baths all around. It was all done by hand with just the one tap in the wash-house. She'd light the boiler and keep stoking it to get the water to boil. She used to wash for the doctors and all the big-wigs. And for the Cliff Hotel

which was very select in those days. Only people who had money went there and not many did have money in those days. When Dad was alive he used to have this pony-trap thing and these people, here, used to hire it from him when they came to stay at the Cliff every year, from London. They brought the Nanny and the Governess and their children, and they'd use it to go off for a ride every day.

Father's on the left in that big picture of the Cliff (48). He was the carrier who brought Mr Gough when he first came here from Bristol, they came in his big waggon and Dad counted them off, one, two three until the last one got down and there was Mrs Gough with her two tin

trunks and an umbrella. Mother often told me about that. When Father first started he had a horse drawn covered-waggon like the cowboys had. He used to go in and out of Bristol with furniture or vegetables and things like that. I used to go with him sometimes when he went down to Wedmore to buy hens. They didn't keep them after the first year when they'd finished laying and Father would take a big coop down and bring 'em back alive. Then he'd kill 'em and Mum would pluck 'em and get 'em ready to sell. He'd buy 'em fer a shillin' and sell 'em fer one an' sixpence. I remember Gert and me went down there once and there was some old lady down there at Clewer — Cocklake Dungeon — an' she gave us a puddin' an' said it was Cocklake-Dungeon-roly-poly-kiddie-puddin', an' whenever we had a roly-poly after that that's what t'was called. Bin called that fer more'n 85 years now."

"Ah yes, these two were a pair from down Wedmore way. That's Jimmy Rogers — Jimmy Shiner — and his wife and his cider barrel. They used to come up here every Saturday to sell their peat. They had their round almost like a milkman — go round the doors and sell a basket at a time, 20 or 30 or whatever people could afford. We used it. It certainly burnt bright and gave off a good heat, and it was lovely smelling stuff. The only trouble was the ashes were very light and, if you got a draught when you opened a door a bit quick, t'would fly all over the house. That peat there is flung out down at the drying centre ready to put in their cart — they had that spring cart with the railings all round 'cause, being so light, they could pile the peat up really high. It was so much easier to haul that up here than to fetch coal from Chilcompton, and that's what I used to do when I was a boy. You'd get half a ton for ten bob in those days."

"At one time a lot of folk cycled down to Cheddar for their Sunday outing. When I was ten or eleven years old four or five of us would go down there together. I could never get over the views. You don't get the beauty of it going down 'cause you've got your eye on the road and you don't get that lovely impression. But walking back! Then you are able to look up and it makes your tummy turn over. Those were the days when the ladies wore their big straw hats and had their skirts tied down so's they wouldn't ride up when their knees were going round. Used to thread their bootlaces through little holes in their skirts. Grandfather got quite vexed when the shorter skirts came in, used to say, *"Was a time when we'd get prosecuted for linen lifting, but now there's no linen there to lift!"* "

Cheddar Village. W5616.

"The water runs under the bridge in the gardens of the Cliff Hotel, doesn't it? Well, I'd cycled down there once when I was a schoolboy and I was in there when there was a bit of a showman there, and he was out to get some easy money off the visitors. He had this rope in his hands and he was offering to show folk his water otter that was down under the bridge. Well, a party of Welsh people turned up and when this chap had collected enough money he pulled his rope in and on the end of it he had a copper kettle! T'was a water 'otter all right 'cause he used it to heat his water, but he dropped his aitch when he said it. But then, when they realised that he'd made a fool of them they picked him up and flung him straight in the water. That was great fun for me to see him go headlong."

"Oh, bugger me, where on earth did you find that one? That's Fred Harris, Victor Chew and Jack Moss — me. Victor is the one who had the water otter. He were the comedian. He'd put his hat down on the ground and rattle the chain and thrash about in the water with his mop stick, shoutin', *"Back a bit! Back a bit!"* not to let them get too close. Then he'd drag this kettle up and say, *"That's otted many a quart o' water."* He made pounds from visitors what came on the coaches.

I went to work at the Cliff Hotel in 1908, when I was twelve. Buttons, I was, stood at the door with me blue uniform with the brass buttons all down the front. Always used to take a pride in being smart and tidy. I used to receive people and take their luggage up to their bedrooms. They'd arrive with their horse and carriage, or on one of the brakes — remember Cigarette

Joe in his straw hat from Weston? And Jimmy Coles? Oh, the Cliff was always full in those days. People would come from all over the place to spend their holidays there.

In 1914, right at the start of the war, I put me age on and joined the army. My father served for a good many years and I wanted to join. There were recruitin' meetin's goin' on all the time and some toff or other — Colonel Yatman, Magistrate — was givin' a pound to anyone who would join up, so I took the pound and went down to Taunton with Harry Brooks. Joined the Somerset Light Infantry. I was in France with them — the 6th Battalion.

First thing we saw when we got there were notices, *"Keep your heads down! Snipers!"* I said to the Colonel, *"Look, I don't want no bloody fightin' here!"* Ha! We were on the Somme — in and out of Delville Wood. We had a bad time there. Then, after a bit, I got moved to the Devons and went to Salonika with them. Lost a lot there, too. After that we went to Bulgaria and when they surrendered we crossed the Danube into Romania to help put King Ferdinand back on the throne. We were the first British soldiers ever to set foot in Bucharest.

I was one of the lucky ones in the war — came through it all unscathed. Harry Brooks came back, too, but he was badly injured. More than 40 men from Cheddar never came back. Rodney Stoke, just up the road, was one of the 'Thankful Villages', they were the lucky ones where all the men who went off to the war came back again. Only 31 of those villages in the whole of England and, would you believe it, seven of them are in Somerset. That's amazin'. Somerset lost thousands and thousands of men; the Somerset Light Infantry alone lost over four and a half thousand.

When I came back to the Cliff I took charge of the bars. Sometimes a gentleman might say to me, *"What about a nice trout for the morning, Mr Moss?"* They knew I could always get one. The water ran under my cellar at the hotel and I had a hole in the floor-board and I did put a bit of cheese on a hook and lower it down. Course, they did go for cheese, t'waddn' fair fishin', that line wouldn't be down more than two minutes and there'd be a trout on the end. Lovely trout — pound and a half, maybe. The place was always busy. Do you know, we once served 1000 teas in one afternoon out in the gardens. Oh, it's lovely to see you, you know, to go back and talk about the normal days, 'stead of these uncivilised times."

Tea Gardens, Cheddar. W5614.

"When I was a lad Cheddar was a peaceful place apart from the news of the Zulu War. I first saw the light of day in September, 1872, when it was still a quiet, rambling place where horses and carts rumbled along uneven roads. Nothing much happened except when the Artillery Column of soldiers with horses halted for refreshment on their way to their training centre. That was an event always hailed with wonder and pride. Our favourite playground at that time was the space outside St Andrew's Church, where we played rounders or kickstone. We would always have a pocketful of marbles and glass alleys with colouring inside, and then there were the iron hoops, the girls having the lighter wooden ones. And who could forget the nutting? Conkers, walnuts and sweet chestnuts; we knew all the trees and their ripening times.

Before six o'clock in the morning I would often make my way down to the milking on Cheddar Moor, passing Annie and Elsie Ford already busy. They lived at Manor Farm. Womenfolk were not too particular about their dress and wore their skirts down to their ankles but, come the Sabbath, and they'd all turn out in a wonderful array of silks and satins and lace trimmings, and hats all covered with flowers and feathers.

A little further along I would cross the river on a narrow plank where William Dean looked after the retorts, which gave a supply of gas to the village. I could get some nubs of limestone there for tuppence, which was enough to do out and whitewash all our walls and leave enough to do the apple trees in the spring.

We made our cider at Church Farm where Jim Rogers lived for many years. I let many a cabbage stump down through the apple mill while the two big revolving wheels were grinding the apples into pulp. When the pulp was ready it was placed in big horse-hair parcels called cheeses and when these reached the top of the press it was screwed down to force out all the juice. And that tasted delicious when it was sucked through a straw. In the early spring I used to set up seed potatoes, or 'chetties', and when they were grown they would be packed into three-peck baskets and covered with the haulms which were forced down tightly by two withy sticks. I once rode through the night with George Totton to deliver these potatoes to Bristol Market. We lay out on top of the baskets and only stopped once, at the pub halfway up Redhill, to rest the horses and get refreshments.

Blacksmiths did a thriving trade in those days and we would often stop to watch the shoeing at Mr Gibson's forge in North Street. I can almost smell now the stench of the red hot shoe when it was fitted to the horse's hoof. Then there was Roper Parsons in the same street. He would take a bundle of hemp under his left arm and walk backwards away from a spindle turned by his lad. He would make any size of rope that you wanted. In those days my pocket money was a penny-ha'penny a week and I would always take it to buy a pound of dates from Alfred Hill at Venn's grocery shop. At Christmas time that place was a feast for us boys to set eyes on with its displays of raisins and currants and so on, with sugar pigs and holly and white wadding scattered about to represent snow.

At William Small's cheesemongery 60lb truckles were common. Mr Small became an expert cheese taster in 1885 and went on to sample over three million cheeses. He'd put in his auger and pull out a plug for his customers to taste and then put what was left back and seal it with his thumb. He used to sell good ripe Cheddar cheese for sevenpence a pound. Grandmother used to make 10lb truckles and throw in a sprinkling of caraway seeds which gave it a distinctive bite. Then she would scald cream and let it rise in round, shallow pans. This was then stored until it turned, and then the butter, which was shaped like a pudding basin, was stamped with a design, placed on a dish with dock leaves over, and covered with a clean white cloth and taken to Mr Lewis, the baker by Cheddar Cross, who sold it at sevenpence a pound.

GAZETTE
CHEDDAR THE CROSS

In those days Cheddar consisted to a large extent of thatched dwellings with most chimneys open to the sky and the chimney-sweep's lad would take off his boots and his socks and clamber up the chimney, scraping it clean as he went. On reaching the top he would stand with his hands on his hips and cry, *"All-one up!"* for all to hear. Local lads were allowed a £10 apprentice-ship to learn trades like carpentry or blacksmithying but they were only allowed a shilling a week for the first year and one and sixpence the second.

There were hard times for many who could not find work or were unable to work. Poor relief amounted to a mere half-crown weekly to keep body and soul together. It was either that or the work-house. There was a charity for the poor who received a pair of sheets one year and a blanket the next.

The political parties in Cheddar were the 'reds' and the 'blues' and in 1892 a Radical candidate was chased from a meeting in Ford's Field and took refuge in the Bath Arms. The angry mob then broke every window in the place, but by the time the police arrived from Axbridge they had disappeared and the candidate had escaped through a back door.

Speaking of violence you must have heard of Jack Plumley the highwayman who lurked with his horse in the small caves to avoid capture. In the old days they always used to hang wrongdoers at Hangman's Rock at the top of Shute Hill, and I understand that highwaymen were buried under the sycamore on the north side of Cheddar Church. It's dark there and it is a tradition that no-one shall be buried there.

In my day the church choir-stalls were fully filled by men and boys. Blind Arthur Allsop was organist there for fully 40 years. He was known for his kindness and did much good work. At Christmas time the vicar always provided a festive feast for the choir, and the children would go to the Vicarage door after the afternoon service to be given a bun and an orange. My grandfather, Jesse Brooks, was sexton for 29 years and on January 6th, old Christmas Eve, he would entertain the bell ringers. At ten they would ring a couple of peals and then a special sort of biscuit was toasted before a huge kitchen fire, dropped into an earthenware pot of hot cider, and served with hot cheese. It was delicious. Then there would be singing of the old-fashioned Cheddar carols and others, until maybe four in the morning, but before they began, a half-gallon, two-handed cider cup was passed around filled with

half cider and half hot gin, and printed on the side were the words:

'Let the wealthy and great roll in splendour and state,
I envy them not, I declare it.
I eat my own lamb, my chicken and ham,
I shear my own fleece and I wear it.
I have lawns I have bowers, I have fruit I have flowers,
The lark is my morning alarmer.
So jolly boys, now — here's God speed the plough!
Long life and God speed the farmer!'

What times, what pleasant memories! Happy days indeed, did we but know."

"This is Sally Spencer, comin' down the gorge, she'd bin somewhere fetchin' somethin', I expect. She was a dear old soul; worked in the laundry for the shirt mill when it was there. Back up behind there, on the left, there was Rowland Pavey's flour mill. There was a big wood behind our cottage when we were kids, and we kept hens there, and we'd come up to Mr Pavey's mill for corn to feed them. That Indian corn made all the difference to the colour of their eggs — a beautiful golden colour. They were really eggs that they laid in those days — now, they're so insipid I don't like them at all. Old Rowland was a funny, eccentric sort of a bloke — did I ever tell you about how he used to draw cartoons? Well, on the other side of the road, there, was his tea rooms, and in the summer the brakes used to either drop their people at the Cliff Hotel or at Pavey's Tea Rooms, and they'd have their lunch or whatever it might be.

And the menu was all written up on the board outside. But then, when the winter came, he'd be at a loose end, and where the menu was written in the summer he'd draw a different cartoon every day. As kids, before we had dinner, we always had to nip up and see what the new cartoon was. He it was who built that Jacob's Ladder, they used to charge a penny each to go up — 300 or something steps. Worth ten bob not to have to climb up! Course, as kids we'd go up over the Lippiatt and come down by his ladder — you were all right as long as you never got caught — but if you did get caught you had to pay at the bottom! He used to have a restaurant thing at the top and he'd put hot meals in a hay box at the bottom and then winch them to the top."

"Rowland Pavey was a very picturesque old fellow, just like Grandfather, and clever too. He was quite a good water-diviner and wrote his own book about it. When he'd mastered that skill he became convinced that he had the ability to see magnetic forces at work. To begin with he reckoned to see them in the earth, but then, with his super-penetrating gaze — what he called his Pantoscopic Faculty — he decided he could see magnetic waves passing through people's bodies. And it was then that he first realised that we all had invisible wings! He was quite convinced of it, though he had to admit that even with his incredible powers they were only faintly visible! He was a great pal of Grand-father Gough's and one year, when Grandfather strung some coloured lights across the

Gorge for some jubilee or another, Rowland took one look and decided that if Grandfather could light it, then he could fly it. He set to and made himself a set of wings out of whalebone and whaleskin — where he got it from goodness only knows, but he strapped the contraption onto himself in such a way that he could pump the things up and down with his arms. Then he went up on his hill — Pavey's Hill — where there was a place called the Ivy Chair — called Preaching Rock as well, 'cause some of the old parsons used to preach up there — anyway, he went up just below the Ivy Chair and jumped off. But all's he did was to fall down some way and land in some scrub and bushes and scratch himself. And that was that. He never tried it again. He was a lovely old character, was Rowland."

"That's the staff of the shirt factories that used to be here. Two of my sisters are on there. Round 1900 I used to take a jug of tea into 'em at four o'clock, then they'd work on till six. Start at eight in the morning, they did. Edie used to do the ironin', and if the passer-out found the slightest speck on a shirt it would go back into the wash. Course, a lot of the finishing off was done in people's homes, in the villages round Cheddar. A manager used to go out to various centres and distribute things and collect what had been done. They'd do bits like fitting the collars, and the sleeves, and putting in button holes. One woman I knew of could make as many as 140 button holes a day. And for that they used to get 2/6d or 2/9d for a dozen finished shirts. It was a great loss to the whole district when they closed up and moved to Taunton."

"At the turn of the century all the mills in Cheddar went flop, and there was a tremendous amount of migration from here to America. My Grandfather's brother was one of those who went and I have a cousin over there whose job meant travelling around checking this and that. One day he found himself in a place in New York State with the extraordinary name of Skaneatles and that was where the immigrants from this area had settled. He found lots of local names and in seeking out one old chap from Draycott he was directed to an orchard. Well, having walked through this avenue of apple trees, which might have come from Somerset, there, in a shed at the bottom of an American garden, he found the village lads, all speaking with Mendip accents and drinking cider from their two handled mugs. On that Sunday morning it was as though nothing whatsoever had changed."

"This is a get-together of the doctors and their friends and families — down at the Nye, probably. There's Doctor Openshaw with little Copper sittin' in front of him, and Victor Clark. And there's Doctor Statham — Reginald Whiteside Statham — the bald headed man sittin' by his mother. Dr Statham brought up half the poor people in Cheddar. He'd give 'em this an' give 'em that. Used to keep cows and he'd give 'em their milk. If there was a child sufferin' from TB he'd say, *'Don' give them any of your milk. Send 'em down to my house an' have it from my cows.'* And they'd go down there with their jugs after the skimmed milk — any amount of 'em. Some of them people were in business, and a lot of 'em were fathers in the pubs, spendin' the housekeepin' money — and he were givin' their youngsters his milk. A marvellous man. They were proper doctors, then, mind you."

"Ah, Lt.-Col. Openshaw. Doctor. Second-in Command the 1st/4th Somersets. Came to India with us in 1914. Very nice chap. Died in '17 from heart failure in Mespot. His son was with us too. We shared quarters in Jullunder before he left us in '15 to join the RFC."

"That's Copper Openshaw he's talking about — in the Flying Corps. A ginger-haired fellow. He had his own aeroplane, a little thing, and he knew how to rise and land, and that's the kind of thing he used to do. Planes were very rare in those days and all we kids knew his. He'd hover over Cheddar for a bit and we'd say, *"Thass Copper again"*, and then he'd come down onto the landing ground by his house. They do say that he once flew in at one end of Cheddar station and out the other. There, I remembered that all right, didn't I!"

Waterfall

"Mother had seven of us, but we always had everything we wanted as a family when I grew up as a kiddie. We lived in several different cottages while I was growing up in Draycott. We always had a big garden or rented land where Father would grow our own vegetables. We'd keep what we needed and sell the rest. We had hens, too, an' what eggs we wanted we did keep for ourselves an' then the rest we'd take to the shop an' swap fer groceries. You didn' know what they were worth till you got them there — if there were a glut on you didn' make so much. The man at the shop would count them an' hold em' up to see there were none cracked. Sometimes we did pay money as well an' sometimes we'd get money back as well as groceries. T'was barter really. Then, when we'd sorted out what we needed, he'd take a piece of paper an' roll it into a cone shape an' pop a few sweets in an' give us with the top curled down.

We always kept a pig — most everybody did in those days — an' when he were fat enough we'd have'n killed by the butcher. What he used to do were kill'n an' let the blood come out, an' then roll'n onto a bed of straw an' set fire to the straw, tuh burn all the hair off'n. I know some people did use that blood tuh rub into their wooden panellin' in ther houses, tuh keep the rich colouring, an' thass the truth. When the pig was scraped clean the butcher ud put a gambrel through the sinews of his hind legs an' hang'n up an' cut it from top to tail. He'd catch all the innards in a bucket an' sell 'em fer sixpence tuh make faggots. Mother ud use up all the inside while it were fresh — use up the pork an' that — an' then salt the bacon an' the hams. Some people used to rub in brown sugar an' ground barley an' all sorts to give it a sweet taste but Mother just used to use salt an' saltpetre, an' when t'was done t'was hung up in the kitchen to keep. That were delicious. Sometimes when we did come home from school we 'ould take the sharp knife an' cut off a rasher of that bacon an' eat it raw where it tasted so good.

Most of Mother's cookin' were done on the open fire, or what they did call a Yorkshire range — we did call'n the Lime Kiln. He had an oven on one side, the open fire in the middle, an' a little place on t'other side where you did put yer stick tuh dry, tuh light next mornin'. You'd put yer stick in the oven, an' get'n hot, an' then brush it all out an' mop it round an' then put yer bread in where the fire had just come out. Then the iron door were shut fer the bread tuh bake. When t'was ready you could lift the bread out an' pull all the little bits of wood an' ash off — but t'was smashin' bread. An' no shortage of butter. Near enough every farmer made butter — some would have a cow-shaped pattern on the top, or it might be a rose — pressed in with a wooden mould.

Dad always got his cider made. Nearly everybody had a few apple trees and pretty well everybody kept cider. Then they did all go out visitin' Sunday mornin's. There were a number of farms round here where three or four chaps would get together of a Sunday in them days. Then, come haymakin' time, they'd all turn out tuh help the farmer. Dad always kept his in the backhouse. Always kept a hoxid er so — a hogshead that is, but we duh cut the corners a bit. Thass fifty-four gallons. That did last accordin' to how quickly you did drink it, an' how many you did get visitin'. But when Dad's barrel were out he did always know where to get someone else's. Mother never drank, she were teetotal all her life.

Every Sunday mornin' we kiddies had to 'ave a spoonful of brimstone an' treacle. There were a great basin full o' the stuff mixed up in a thick paste, an' we'd take our turn an' twist the spoon round and round not for the treacle to run off. That cleaned yer insides out. Every Sunday.

Now, I'm gonna tell you a little story what happened to me in my younger days that you wouldn't hardly believe. The school doctor come round an' said I had tonsils and adenoids want doin'. I were about seven years old as I should judge now. Dr Statham an' Dr Openshaw come an' seen me mother an' decided that they'd operate me on such an' such a day at home on the kitchen table. They said, *"See that he doesn' have nothin' to eat that day"*. So there I am,

not havin' tuh go tuh school — that were the best part — an' Mother givin' me nothin' to eat. But walnuts were about at that time so I did stroll off an' pick up these things an' eat without Mother knowin'.

Then they came fer the operatin'. I can picture them now, leavin' their horses by the shop at the bottom an' George Hale lookin' after them while they come in. They came up the path an' in. All's I had on were a shirt an' they led me down on the table an' stuck this thing over me nose an' put chlorry-form on an' put me tuh sleep. They done the operation. Fer several days afterwards I had this shirt on an' they'd wasted a bit of this chlorry-form, let a drop fall on me shoulder, an' I couldn' leave that alone — I had tuh smell it. An' that made I as sick as a dog.

An' fer all their operatin' on me mother's kitchen table they never made no job of it, 'cause me tonsils grew agen an' me adenoids grew agen. An' they never knew nothin' about the walnuts what I'd pinched.

And here's another thing what happened wie me. One day when I were five or six years old I'd saved up enough coppers tuh go tuh Cheddar on the train. Course, we left our mothers a bit younger in them days than what they do now — wouldn' be trusted on a train nowadays. Anyway, t'were about a penny fer the couple o' miles in. I'd never bin on a train in me life an' by the time we got into Cheddar I'd got a bit upset an' I were taken short. T'were a penny tuh to go inuh the toilet an' I expect I hadn' much left so it went against the grain, but I had tuh go in.

In those days all's we had in our cottages fer a lavatory were a wooden seat wie a big hole fer grown-ups an' a little one fer children — side by side, an' they had either buckets underneath what had to be emptied or a pit that was seen to every now and agen. Thass all we ever had. Anyway, I went intuh this one on the station, an' that was another penny gone. I did what I had tuh do an' was pullin' up me trousers when I saw t'was wrote there, *"Please pull the flush"*. An' I pulled'n, trousers half up an' half down. Didn' know what were gonna happen an' then this water started rushin' down an' I thought I'd broke the bugger. I hared outa there, doin' up me trousers as I ran down the platform. That were in Cheddar.

I started school on me third birthday and ran away one day afterwards. I didn' care much for it. I were told what to do if I wanted to go to the toilet — you had to ask to leave the room, an' I thought, well, thass where me bloomin' hat is. I wen' out, got me hat, an' buggered off home. In them days you'd start from babies an' leave from the same school. An' it was a mile walk. A mile to school, a mile home to dinner an' another two mile in the afternoon. Three year old! An' at some schools you had to take tuppence each Monday to pay fer your lessons an' if you forgot you'd be sent home to fetch it. I left school when I were twelve, under the agricultural policy of 1913. If you were in the top standard for one year you could go to Wells an' take an exam; an' if you passed you could leave; or go to the Grammar School if your parents could afford it. Well, wie seven of us in the family, mine couldn'. Six from my class went fer the exam together. That was on the Saturday.

Well, the Post was a bit different then to what it is now — must have bin, 'cause when I went tuh school on Monday mornin' the postman had bin. The schoolmaster said, *"Now silence."* An' he read out the letter what said who had passed an' who 'adn'. I had. I said, "When can I leave?" He said, *"Whenever you like"*. I said, "Cheerio!" went out to the lobby, picked up me hat, an' set off home.

Goin' down towards our cottage I had to pass a butcher's house what I used tuh work with sometimes — Saturdays. He said, *"Hello you bugger, you've runned away agen!"* I said, "No, I've left." He said, *"Jump up then."* He was off with his cart, deliverin' round the villages. I got home at six o'clock. I were on a good thing. Started work, an' half-a-crown a week."

CHEDDAR POST OFFICE
G.R.HILL
CADBURY'S
CHOCOLATE
POST OFFICE
FOR
MONEY ORDER SAVINGS BANK
PARCEL POST TELEGRAPH &
INSURANCE AND ANNUITY BUSINESS
LLOYD'S
TEA
LETTER BOX

"In the low country, on the other side of Mendip Hills, lies Cheddar; before the village is a large green, or common, a piece of ground, in which the whole herd of cows belonging to the town, do feed; the ground is exceeding rich, and as the whole village are cow keepers, they take care to keep up the goodness of the soil, by agreeing to lay on large quantities of dung for manuring and enriching the land, the milk of all the town cows is brought together every day in a common room where the persons appointed measure every man's quantity, and set it down in a book; when the quantities are adjusted, the milk is all put together, and every meal's milk makes one cheese, so that the cheese is bigger, or less, as the cows yield more, or less, milk. By this method the goodness of the cheese is preserved and, without all dispute, it is the best cheese that England affords, if not, that the whole world affords."

Daniel Defoe 1725

Mr Small, Expert Cheddar Cheese Taster For Nearly 50 Years.

"Cheddar cheese is proper cheese an' nobody don' eat more'n it than I do; I were brought up on it. Me mother an' me aunties were all champion cheesemakers. Aunt Clessie won prizes fer hers in London. Great 96lb cheeses she used to make an' never let a man carry one of 'em. Said they'd bang the edges about an' spoil 'em. Always kept men out of her dairy. An' she were at it every day mind, Sundays an' all; didn' make no difference what day it were. I got an idea, an' Mother always said, that Cheddar cheese is best 'cause they didn' fiddle wie it. T'is made as should be made an' that's why t'as took on so much. If you'm puttin' the right ingredients in you don' 'ave tuh worry about it, t'will turn out properly. Same as everythin' else — once you duh start fiddlin' wie it tuh make summit different, you'm gone off of real Cheddar cheese.

Years an' years ago farmers used tuh make their own cheese. My grandfather did. They always reckoned that June were the best month for the best cheese 'cause there was certain times of the year, July till the beginning of August, when the buttercups is about and the milk is rich and that did send it sort of sourified; you know, make the cheese taste bitter. Then perhaps you'd have to get up at two o'clock in the bloomin' mornin' tuh get it started off. Then, as the year did go on, the buttercups did die out and the milk'd get better. 'Tis all accordin' tuh the weather, see, and you gotta be very careful 'cause all sorts of things do affect the cheese. If the cows is ill it'll affect the milk an' when you're cheese makin' you don't dare to eat onions, the smell do get right into the cheese. Look, when my mother changed her job for a better un, £80 a year an' her livin' for makin' a 100-cow dairy cheese, she had tuh sign tuh say she wouldn' smoke or eat onions or peppermints or anythin' like that.

Mother used tuh make 200 gallons a day at one time when she was up on the Mendips. That were Mother's and Father's milk, Grandfather's and another farmer's, topside, by the name of Towle. All three of their milks used to go together to make up the amount. She used tuh start at seven if the weather was right, making last night's milk up today. To start with she did put it all in a 200 gallon copper and heat it up to a temperature with a wood fire. Then she'd put some rennit in it and so quick as that did get on the turn she would break it wie a breaker wie a long handle, like a pitchfork only with irons goin' the other way as well to make squares. When that did get to a certain thickness she did drain off the whey which did go to the pigs, and there were the cheese, left in the bottom like gurt slabs of icecream.

After that Mother 'ud salt it an' break it an' cut it up and put it in vats — little round things — 8lb, 12lb, 16lb. They'm like little cocoa tins. You've seen a truckle cheese, surely. Well, they'm made by puttin' the cheese in these little tins an' then screwin' it down for tuh press it. Then that 'ad tuh bide a while fer the whatsit, the superfluid, tuh drain away afore they were put in muslin an' taken into the cheese room. When it was there it had tuh stay fer six months an' be turned every day. When t'were ready the farmer 'ud have what he needed an' then some 'ud be sold from the farm 'an some taken tuh market. Sometimes a proper man 'ud come with a skewer thing an' pull a plug o' cheese to try it afore he bought it. P'raps come from a big store or the Co-op.

When we were all young, Mother couldn' leave the cheese tubs tuh see us. When the cheese were fast she had tuh be there. In addition tuh the cheese there were a baker's ub'n where the fire were to, an' she did have tuh bake her own bread when the fire were goyn. We used tuh go in an' say, *"Mam, we'm hungry. We wan' summit tuh eat."* An' if the curd was forward enough she'd hit a piece off an' say, *"Ere, push this in thee mouth an' geddon out. I ab'n got time tuh play withee now."* They 'ad tuh work for ther livin' in them days. She 'ad a hard damn life, mind, ain't no two ways about it."

"We used to be famous for cheese at Brice's. E.B. Brice was our grandfather; Busson Brice. Great-grandmother was a Huguenot and that was the name of the French side of the family. That's Grandfather in the middle of the picture. He had a very good business in those early days — he sold everything. There was the drapery on one side and grocery on the other, and opposite there was the hardware — linoleum and things. The place over there had been a public house once — Buck House — before Father had it altered into a shop. Eventually he sold it to the India and China Tea Company.

Our cheese room was up a ladder and all around the shelves were great big truckles that Father would buy from the farmers. As well as the cheese store we had a bacon house, a tea room and

a sugar house. We had to keep them apart so's they didn't take the other smells on. The sugar was all kept in bins — it wasn't sold in packets then. It was all weighed up in little red bags or blue bags. Father bought them in hundreds — different colours for different types of sugar.

An enormous number of people depended on us for their supplies and Father used to go all round the countryside collecting their orders. He'd go off with Kitty pulling his high-standing trap — it would be a special honour for us to go as well 'cause Kitty was a rather flighty horse. The Lympsham journey was once in three weeks and so was the Brent, but Wells was more frequent — then there were Charterhouse and Burrington and the other places. Father would call at the same cottages and farms regularly and supply everything his customers needed in the grocery way, and everything they needed in the drapery way — baby clothes, the lot. He'd collect the orders and then the long carts went out to deliver them. On Saturdays he went to Wookey Hole, and then our sister Molly would go with him to help."

"Yes, I did that for about ten years when I was a little girl. We were a long family and I was the last girl. I was very fond of Father all my life and, like Christopher Robin had to take care of his mother, I had to look after Father. I couldn't let him down. I couldn't let him go out all alone in miserable weather. We'd get soaking wet, but I'd never let him go alone. We'd go off in the tiny little cart which Mr Alfred Scorse built for Tommy, the little Exmoor pony, with Father and me bobbing along on this little wooden seat. The whole thing was like a little square box on wheels with a plank seat laid across. We'd go through all the villages and end up at Wookey Hole, and everywhere we stopped I'd wait with the pony and trap while Father went into the cottages for the orders. It was mighty hard work for him. He'd come back from his journeys and then have to total up the cash register last thing at night, but on Saturday night at twelve o'clock he'd come out of the shop, lock the door, and not go back again until Monday morning. Sunday was the only day Father had with his family when we were little, and on Sundays we went to church.

I can see Father now, wearing his top hat and frock coat to chapel, they always wore beautiful plush top hats in those days. Father kept his in a lovely leather box. He'd come down rubbing round his hat with a pure silk, cream handkerchief — it had to be pure silk mind! In those days it was all top hats. And Brice's would supply those too. And widow's weeds and suits for funerals. People always wore black for funerals and the machinists who lived over the shop would make everything they needed. Brice's used to do everything for the country people. It was a very go-ahead business back in Grandfather's day.

Every year we all used to go up and have a lovely time in the haymaking field at West Acre. Everyone used to come to help and to have a picnic. We'd invite our friends from the village and our cousins from Bath and everyone who was employed in the business would come. Mr Burgess, who worked in the shop is there, and Miss Evans in the dark skirt, who was our

housekeeper and Miss Cole, who used to look after us — 'cause there were eight of us in those days. Mother and Father are on the right and Jim Simmonds, next to them, who used to look after the horses. After the Great War they got a Ford van and Jim went to work up at the caves.

When the grass was cut and ready, we children had to rake it up and put it up in cocks. Then it would all be put up on those waggons — the ones they used to deliver the groceries on — and it would all be taken to the loft near the shop and kept there for the horses. When it was all cleared from the field the horses would be put back. Then, in the evening, we'd all go back to our kitchen and everyone would sit around the great kitchen table and have tea with us. It was a big house and a big family."

"Now, I wouldn't tell you nothin' rude — not fer the life of me, but I'm talking to you the same as I would to me mates down the pub. Now, fer a start, I'm not a Cheddar man. I came here to work in March, Ladyday, 1914, from Draycott — two miles away, but I'm told I'm still not a Cheddar man. I'm an outsider — a Draycott bloke.

Now then, what I'm gonna tell you is the truth, and there are still people round here who'll tell you it's the truth. When I were a young man there used tuh be an old muddy ditch run all up alongside the road where I did live — it were two er three foot wide an', on average, about the same deep wie mud; 'cause there was a bit of a stone weir there to keep the mud from goin' in the pond.

Well, in those days I used tuh go out every Tuesday night, drinkin' and playin' cards in the Butcher's Arms — they useda have an extension in them days till 11 o'clock. Always useda drink cider then, before I had more sense. I don't now, 'cause that duh rot thee socks. Any'ow, I'm down there one night — a hell of a cold and wet night — an' this chap who was wie us put on his overcoat an' went out tuh post a letter off tuh somebody er another.

We wen' on wie our card playin' an' then, after a bit, young Herbie comes in an' says to me, *"Jake, he who went out just now is in the river!"* I said, "Best o' luck to'n," an' went on playin' me hand — I thought he were pullin' me leg, see. Then the barman comes over an' sez, *"Young Herbie is worried, mind. T'is true what he's sayin"*.

In the circumstances I said "All right" an' I drank up an' wandered out an' said, "Where's the bugger to, then." *"In 'ere, look!"* Well, in that ditch t'were all reeds an' rushes, right up high — an' animal muck. Thass all t'were along the side o' the road. I looked in an all's I could see were the top of 'is bloody bald 'ead — his hat were gone, but there was 'is bald head. He still had this gurt coat on, an' the more he struggled the more he did go down in. Well, I 'ad a bit of tidy on fer a change, fer me night out, an' I weren't gonna get it dirty not fer he ner nobody else, so I bent down an' caught hold of'n by the arm an' pulled. 'Schhllup', the mud did go — an' we couldn't pull'n out. He were a dead weight an' thik gurt coat were pullin'n down in further.

About then I started tuh get the wind up, an' I told Herbie tuh go an' get his liddle car, so's we could tie that'n on'n. Whilst he were gone I got down a bit further — but I weredn't gonna get in wie'n, not even if the bugger died! Well, Herbie come back an' we put the car so's the lights were pointin' to the ditch — 'cause t'were as dark as a bag. Then we hitched a rope round his arm an' onto the car. Then I said, "Pull steady."

All of a sudden I could hear runnin' down the road. The barman must've called *"Time"* at the pub — an' then they could all come out to help. Two on 'em come down all dressed up — I were a bit tidy but they 'ad proper suits on an' everythin'. They said, *"Whass on, Jake?"* An' I said, "I'm pullin' the bugger out wie the car. I've 'ad one go at'n, but can't get'n out very well. Can't let Herbie drive very fast, see." Then they said, *"'Ang on, you'm gonna pull 'is bloody arm out."* An' I said, "Well, t'is no use left in there. The bugger'll get freezed."

So they said, *"Thass no good"*, an' took the rope off the car an' give it to me. An' then, would you believe it, they got in wie'n! Got in all thik muck! Bugger me if I were goin' to! Well, eventually they dragged him out wie their arms all around him an' we stuck him on the side o' the road, an' I said, "Let the bugger bide there an' drain out." Then, after a bit, off we goes to his home, wi' they with their arms still round 'im, cuddlin' 'im, an' me pushin' from the back, out the way o' the mud. I thought, "Well, you'm gonna be in a mess, but Jake iddn'." When we gets there we knock on the door an' his mate comes to answer. *"Whass up?"* he sez. *"Oh,"* sez Herbie, grinnin', *"That daft bugger bin an' fell in the river down there."* An' there he were, shiverin' an' shakin', but a bit of life were comin' back into 'is legs.

Awkward stairs they had there, twisty, but up we goes, wie me still be'ind pushin', out the way o' the mud. (This is the best bit comin' now. Put yer fingers in yer ears out there, Missus.) We got the bugger up there an' I said, "Where d'er sleep?" He showed me which bed t'were, showed me some bloody old rags down on the floor — alls he 'ad tuh sleep on. Well, we couldn' leave'n like that so we started undressin'n wie mud an' water still runnin' down the stairs. We got 'is clothes off 'an there he is, whinin', wie his hands protectin' his offendin' parts. *"Oh, no, no! Don' undress me!"* But we 'ad, an — bugger me! — he didn' 'ave nothin' to be proud of! Just like a liddle white slug. An' the cold water adn' 'elped.

In the end we left'n bide there an' we wen' on home. T'other two were in a damn good mess, but I weredn'. Next mornin' I got up an' thought I'd just walk outside an' have a look-see, an' there were his hat, floatin'. I took'n out an' wrung'n out. Then I began tuh get a bit worried about how he were, 'cause I wouldn' 'ave bin surprised if the poor sod had bin dead the state he'd bin in. Should I 'ave sin the police or summit? Well, I wen' up an' wen' in an' there they both were, wie a good fire goin' an' him wie 'is clothes on. The pair on 'em were sittin' dryin' out the wet notes from his wallet. Bugger me! This goin' in your book then? Wanna pinch o' snuff?"

"When I was younger all the country people would go to a pub and either sing or step-dance to make their own entertainment. Those who step-danced would have tips on their boots — anything to make a bit of a row. Bob Starr was a step-dancer — a champion — could dance all night. He reckoned that if he'd had enough to drink he could dance on a pint cup. He'd have a pint of cider in one hand and try to dance on another. He did reckon that in his younger days he did dance on the table and did dance so light that after he'd been goin' fer a bit they could take the table away from underneath him. Then they all had their country songs, things like: *"Come round Cheddar with me, Sing a little, Save a little, Save a little summit fer a rainy day."* I can't remember all on't but that kind o' thing. In those days you made your own enjoyment, and there was a damn sight more then than ever there is now."

"I took more than one of Father's cider barrels round to Cooper Thomas. He'd re-hoop them and get 'em ready for the next lot. Cider was a nice custom — to go round and have a glass with friends. I think everybody in Cheddar had a way of putting a barrel away for their own use. You must have heard how they'd get a hogshead of cider and throw in a great joint of raw beef and that would get eaten away, the bone and all would disappear and give the drink a nice colour. As a matter of fact my father used to boil a saucer full of beetroot, all lovely and red, and stuff them in through the bung-hole. When his pals would come around Sunday mornings for a drop they'd take a bit and say, *"Caw, that's got a good colour, Charlie!"* Father wasn't a boozer, or anything like that, but he always had friends!"

"Father was the village wheelwright, always working in wood. He was the local carpenter as well and, for that reason, the undertaker; and also a builder. We were doing all those things at one time. Then, in the early days, when motor cars became available, the back axle replaced the cart wheel and eventually the pneumatic tyre won the day. The wheelwright retired and was not replaced.

As motor vehicles became more and more common they began rolling off the production line as chassis, with the bodies being built separately, and for about two or three years these chaps who had been working with ash and the like, as wheelwrights, turned their hands to building charabancs. I think they used to turn out about two bodies a week at the old paper mill here. They also used to make a sports car body — our people did the ash work and someone else did

the panel beating. But then the motor industry cottoned on to the idea of doing its own bodywork, and that was that.

For half a century we also made chip baskets for the strawberry trade — a sort of side issue to the carpenters' work. We had a small factory with about a dozen girls who made the baskets. They were really veneers, plaited and stapled together. We used to use Scots pine — a log frame would be sawn into planks and then the chumps guillotined into chips. We made square plaited baskets but there was another chap who did a diagonal weave, and a very handsome basket it was too, but more difficult to make.

The Scots pine had to be used when it was green and wet, you couldn't dry it and stack it and then use it. It had to be felled and used forthwith. And a great drawback was that if it were more than three months old it gradually turned a brown colour which wasn't attractive. By the time I began we had practically denuded the entire area of Scots pine, so we had to look around for a suitable substitute and eventually discovered that Black Poplar was all right for the job. And so the area was stripped of its Black Poplar in the interest of strawberry baskets. After that we used to get part cargoes of Russian aspen, in tow with England's Glory in Gloucester. That produced a white basket that stayed white. But natural resources are running out. It's all plastic now.

First there was the punnet — a little square thing without a handle. Then there was the two pound basket with a bowed over handle, then a four pound and a six pound. The six pound was for the jam fruit at the end of the season. These would be put five in a row with a stick through the handles and bound with binder twine, then they'd be taken to the station and stacked in the waggons and sent to the markets in Sheffield, Birmingham and wherever. For us, the main push came in the spring. In those days growing strawberries was everyman's job. Artisans would have half an acre, or an acre, or an allotment, or whatever, which was down to strawberries, and we would deliver baskets to them from the end of April onwards. At the height of the season I suppose we might move about 40-50 gross of baskets of various sizes in a week."

"When I was a youngster my mother used to make tea for John Coles's strawberry picking staff, working up close to Lion Rock, and we kiddies used to have to take the cans up there for them to have a drink. That would be about 1894 or 5. Then, when I was big enough, I used to go picking for him myself. We'd start at four o'clock in the morning and pick till about eight, then we'd go back up again later in the day. Thruppence an hour. We were well off then, you know. Strawberry season was in June and we used to have three weeks holiday from school for that. That was our holiday — out to work. Summer holidays was for strawberry picking. I'd never eat the things though. Still don't. I hate strawberries. Mind you, raspberries I like."

“We used Scourse’s baskets, but a lot of people did buy the material and make their own up during the winter months. That was our living, growing strawberries. We had a bit of land here and a piece there — perhaps two or three acres. You were on with it all the year round, preparing things and setting them and picking them. We used to grow the Royals and the Nobles — about the only two to start with, then there were the Axbridge Early and the Bradley Cross — all Cheddar names. Nowadays they have to send away for certified stock but when we grew our own we always picked out the blossom. Years ago they used to keep the plants for three years but most of them would hoik them out at two year and replant. And they’d try to plant in fresh ground to give the soil a rest. A good one-year-old, maiden plant put in early will

produce the best fruit the following year. We didn't use glass or anything in those days and we used to bed them down in fern from the Mendips. We'd go up and fetch it down with a dray. You know, strawberry growing only really started in Cheddar about a hundred years ago, some say it was Francis Brooks who started it, but most reckon it was Sam Spencer who used to grow hot-house plants. Anyway, this valley is ideal for them. Blagdon and Ubley, and all round there, the sun just rises and that's all there is to it, but round here t'is more suitable — the Mendips is shielded from the wind, and, when the sun gets round the hills, sort of pens the rays into the gardens for to ripen the fruit. You've got to grow them where the south sun shines all the time. In the old days the picking generally started in June. You could always get somebody

to help you with the picking — at fourpence or fivepence an hour they were glad to. We'd use the housewives — try to keep the kiddies out if we could. In the season we'd take them down to the station. Goodness knows how many trains went from there every week. London, Sheffield, Glasgow — the Strawberry Specials. They carried an incredible amount of strawberries. More than one nursery has picked a whole ton in a single day. They'd all get taken down there piled up in the carts. The smallest baskets were the two pound ones, tied, five on a stick. Then, towards the end of the picking, when they were getting cheaper, we'd put them in four pound baskets — still tied on sticks and heaped up in the station waggons. You'd never think about what they'd look like when they had got to Birmingham or wherever it was they were going. They must have been pretty mushy sometimes!"

"My first job was on that Strawberry Line. Father had always been a Great Western man — started in the 1870s, and I joined on February 2nd, 1905. We were living in Wiltshire then, and I left my home at quarter past six in the morning and went to Bristol to get my orders, and they sent me to Winscombe. Sent as additional staff — a lad porter. Fourteen years old. That was 50 miles away from my home and I knew not a soul in the village. Didn't know the station-master nor the staff on the station. No-one at all. Well, the station-master found me some lodgings and told me where to go and I got fixed up all right. Cost ten shillings a week out of the twelve I made. Twelve shillings a week for 66 hours and happy to do it. Proud of it.

I worked a 12 hour day with an hour off fer the mid-day meal, and half an hour off fer breakfast if you were on early, or the same off fer tea if you were on a later turn. Sundays were extra — but no extra pay, just the weekly rate. Very little Sunday work about then where we were, not like up at Weston. But they had difficulties up there. There were two stations there, the GWR and the Weston, Clevedon and Portishead line — always known as the WC and P. I had one friend there on duty with the GWR one Saturday afternoon when a lady came up who had missed her train to Clevedon. She spotted old Ted and asked him when the next train was. Well, it was not for two or three hours so she asked him if there was anything else she could do. *"Yes,"* he said. *"You can go down the WC and P if you like."* She was livid! But t'was awkward, you see. If only they'd put the damned letters round the other way, PC and W, t'would have bin all right. But they didn't, and t'was always awkward at Weston-super-Mare.

My chief duty when I started was to keep the station clean and give a hand with the other work. When it came to holidays you had to work a whole year first before you got any, and then you got three days off a year. When you'd completed five years it went up to four days. After ten years it became five days, and when you'd been in the service for 15 years you got your first full week's paid holiday. Fifteen years, mind. And the discipline was very strict — but no-body suffered from it, we enjoyed it. When I was a porter I'd never have gone to work with my shoes not shining and buttons cleaned and so on. Everybody took a pride in his job. We obeyed the station-master, we respected his office, his authority. That was the way on the GWR. It really was a tip-top affair and no doubt about it. Oh, the GWR was the best railway in the world!"

"Grandad was the ganger on the Cheddar Valley Line at the end of the last century. Every morning when my dad had milked the cows, he had to take Grandad's breakfast to him in the line hut in Cheddar. Grandma cooked two slices of fried bread and put a piece of fried bacon on one, then a fried egg on that and the rest of the bread on top. If ever Dad slipped on a wet sleeper or something and broke the yolk of the egg he would get sent home to the cottage for his mother to do another one. Grandad got paid one golden sovereign a week, and Dad told us that he always had the imprint of it in the cloth of his back pocket — you could always see it there — and if ever the one was taken out another one would be put in its place. I never knew my Grandad 'cause at the end he led in bed and his toes fell off. And he died. Gangrene."

"Well, did you ever. I know all of them, they're all Mendipers from up Charterhouse way, but they're all gone to rest now. Not a soul of them left alive. That's my mother in the fancy hat, and there's lovely Mrs Lukins, my schoolmistress. Her husband was the gardener at the Nordrach Sanatorium for consumptives. And that's Rev. Lambrick with the buttonhole, he gave this outing. John Coles has brought them down to the station on his brake but I can't remember if they went to the zoo or Bournemouth. These all went to the little church at Charterhouse — we collected money and built it and t'was full every Sunday, but now there's no-body goes. We were all born up there and when I was a little girl I'd pick mushrooms and blackberries to bring down to Cheddar to sell. The minedry was still on the go then — the lead miners were at work. Oh, how nice to see this. Lovely, innit?"

"We didn't live very far from the mineries, either. Have you ever heard the legend that Christ came here once, with his uncle, to fetch lead? That's what some people say. Those miners were tough men, mind, with their own laws. At one time, if any of them stole from his mates, he would be shut up in his wooden cabin and the whole place would be burnt to the ground."

"That was back in the 15th and 16th centuries when that used to happen — not recently. In those days they used to shove the thief into his hut and then pile all the gorse and bracken that they could find around the outside and set fire to it, but the chap inside had his hands and feet free, and if he could break out once it was ablaze he would be allowed to make a run for it. But he was never permitted to return. The last of the mines

shut down sometime around 1905, and the old miners used to tell me that if any of their colleagues was found stealing from them, the man responsible would be transported to Van Dieman's Land, and all his possessions would be burnt — fired. People tell me that the word got to America, 'cause over there, when a man is sacked, they say he's been fired. Well, that word came from the laws of the Mendip lead-miners. And Christ never came here — He had far too much sense to carry that heavy stuff around!"

"We moved to Charterhouse from Ubley when I was three, 'cause Father was a gamekeeper for Mr Gaythorne Hill, the ship owner. All our family belongings were piled up on a waggon and I walked the whole of the three or four miles behind it. Do you know what a three-legged boot-repairing thing is? A heavy metal thing. Well, I carried one of those all the way. Then, within a few months of moving there, my mother died. I remember it quite well — people coming to our house and me hiding round a corner. *"Poor little fellow, what'll happen to him now?"*

After that, Father used to take me about with him. Sometimes we'd go down to Cheddar to buy things. Father would buy a sixty-pound cheese for threepence a pound and then he'd cut it up with a long wire and sell it to our neighbours. Other times we'd walk down to get poison or wire for his traps and things. I remember we often made nets and such in the evenings for catching rabbits. Now and again, Father would go down to one of the pubs in Cheddar for the evening, playing billiards or cards, and I'd keep out of the way in the back kitchen. Then, on our way back up the Gorge it'd be so dark you couldn't see where the sky began. I'd walk with my hand in his pocket — sometimes I needed him and sometimes he needed me — and if we got tired we'd stop for a rest or a nap in the Gorge. We were stopped dozing like that one night when a terrific noise frightened me and woke me up. *"It's only a screech owl,"* said Father.

When I was a lad I used to catch moles along by the mineries — hundreds of them. I'd set my traps in their runs and when I'd caught them I'd take them out and skin them with my knife and put them in my pocket. Dan Lovell, at school, used to get a penny for every mole's tail he had so I'd swap my tails for his skins. I'd get anything up to sixpence for each skin. I'd spread them out and dry them at home and then send them off to London to be made into moleskin coats. I made my first £5 like that. I thought I was the richest man in the country. I was seven or so at the time."

"Old Johnny Cole were comin' down through one afternoon wie three or four ladies in his waggonette, an' Cliff Lane were lookin' over the wall an' said, *"W'art goin', John?" 'Oh,"* he said. *"Down to Burnham." "Well then, wait a minute,"* called Cliff. *"Take my old woman along wid'ee. Burn her an' all."* 'Nother time Johnny was carryin' a pail of milk on his head past Ham's cider house an' somebody threw an apple an' knocked the whole thing right off his head. Just one apple. Caw, Johnny cussed. In those days folk would make up a ring of cloth and walk for miles with their pail balanced on this pad on their head. I can muns see a man by the canal with a seven gallon pail on his head and another tin in each hand. Before the cars were here some of the farmers got bicycles so's they could bring a pail of milk back on each handlebar — but nern on 'em couldn' ride the things!"

"Oh, goodness me, that could very well be me running alongside that brake . My father kept the George there, on the right. You know, there were five other pubs in Axbridge in those days, with probably fewer than 1000 people. Pubs everywhere, and drunks too! Father was a very jocular man — Patsy Lane, they called him — and he had the most popular pub in the village, four bars and an out-business. He used to sell a lot of cider and beer in jars, and the mothers used to come in and buy it for their husbands who couldn't get out. Father's place was always packed with people. He'd always have bread and cheese and pickle and that sort of thing on the table, and there was a concertina — one of those things that go up and down — for the customers to play when they wanted a bit of a sing-song. Trippers used to come to us

from Weston with their brakes and horses and they'd always stop outside our place when they were going to the Gorge. Lots of those people were Welshmen who used to come over from Cardiff and Swansea and land at the old pier in Weston. Father-in-law was the Commodore of the ships that came over — John West. The ships used to ply between Cardiff and Ilfracombe and Weston, and when they got there the brakes would be waiting to bring them to Cheddar. All the world wanted to come to Cheddar.

There was a lavatory up in the garden behind the pub and, as boys, my brother and I used to wait outside for the people to come out. Then we used to stand on our heads for them and hand them roses which we'd been up and pinched from Father's garden, and they'd give us a couple of coppers. That's how we came to get our pocket-money. I must say those Cardiff people were very generous towards us, we used to collect anything up to a shilling. Father wasn't too happy, mind!

Ours was the only stop these brakes made on their way out from Weston, 'cause they needed a pause for their horses to get a breather. All those brakes had names, you know, Britannia was one, and Rosebud, Westward Ho!, things like that. There'd be a chap on the back with a hunting horn and when they got to Tween Town, in Cheddar, he would sound it so that the lads in the Gorge would know to get the chocks ready for the wheels, and the shopkeepers would know they were on their way. When they went back to Weston afterwards they never stopped. They went straight through, and when those horses were galloping with a full load they didn't want to stop. Oh, it was a proper posh affair in the old summer days.

When I left school I served my time doing ironmongery for five years in Bristol, during which time I got two shillings for the first week, four for the second, then six, eight, ten. That was 1908. Father had to keep me in lodgings in there, but I'd cycle home every weekend and by the time I got there I'd either be covered in limestone dust from the roads or, if it was wet, covered in mud. Mud and slosh everywhere.

The day war broke out I was in Maidenhead, working as a junior improver in a hardware store in the main street. There were two of us working together and on the way to work we passed a recruiting office — *'Kitchener needs you'* and all that. We walked in and never came out again — got collared. The governor of the hardware business gave us a golden sovereign each and wished us good luck, and that's how I came to join the army. When I came back I was in hospital blues; was in them for two and a half years after the war 'cause I'd collected some nasty wounds — a bullet through my leg, and my lip ripped open, my teeth knocked out and a bit of my nose cut away by a German bayonet. Hand to hand fighting.

I was wearing the blues when I came here in 1923 to Mr Gibson. He was 84 and wanting to retire from his hardware and smithy business. There were two of us after the place, but he gave me a chance. He said he had something he wanted me to do, and if I could do it the business was mine. He wanted me to cut a key for Cheddar Church. Well, he showed me the vice and

the file and the hacksaw and gave me a burnisher to polish the key. *"If you can cut that key to my liking,"* he said, *"the place is yours."* It was a big key, but simple, and within 20 minutes I had the damn thing finished. I was set up in business. Took over on September 29th, 1923.

That's the place there as it was, and I'm on the left. We closed at eight on weekdays and nine on Saturdays, and the very first thing I sold on my first Monday morning was a galvanised bucket. Tenpence ha'penny — I'll always remember. I sold absolutely everything in the hardware trade — paraffin oil lamps, pots and pans, garden tools, spades, forks, lawn-mowers, all sorts. That what you see in the front is a pig feeder. And hay collectors — hay sweeps we called 'em. We sold the Brenton Hay Sweep, made in Cornwall. I used to buy a dozen at a time and sell

one a week to the farmers as regular as clockwork. We had a wonderful connection with all the farmers round here.

This lot you've got on your picture here were from up around Priddy way, queuing up for their water at the fountain there. They used to bring their horses to us from miles around for their shoeing. There were three other blacksmiths in Cheddar — Spratt in Church Street, Heal and Harris — but how they got on I don't know, they must have had a pretty thin time of it. We seemed to have a monopoly of the horses in those days. On frosty mornings 'twould be nothing to see a dozen or more horses outside waiting to be fitted with frost nails to stop them slipping on the icy roads. Frost nails were chisel shaped so's they could penetrate the ice.

Charlie Clark was our blacksmith — he's holding the wheel in that picture outside my shop. We did any number of wheels every week. Farmers with their hay waggons and traps and putt carts — imagine putting a wheel on a putt cart, mind! Four inches wide and nearly five-eights of an inch thick! Took some heating and some lifting — two of us to get it from the forge and out to the bonding platform on the road. Believe me, we had bonding to do nearly every other day, all the years I was in business. Scourse and Sons, just opposite, were the wheelwrights and they'd make the spokes and felloes and then we'd do the bonding at our place — put the iron tyres on. And we'd repair the axles of the carts. We'd do any repairs connected with iron work — cutting and shotting children's hoops together, helping Cooper Thomas with the hoops for his barrels, all things like that.

Up over the shop was my tinsmith's shop. Up in the Gorge they used to sell truckles of cheese, pound cheeses, small ones — absolutely tasteless, never given time to mature. There were several shops up there selling the stuff, and every Monday morning they'd come down to my place for the tinsmith to put his tins around them so's they could be sent to America, and all over the world, for people who wanted to send them home.

Every cheese they sold was different so we couldn't make a stock size. They had to be packed without any paper, 'cause if they went to tropical places, and the cheese melted, the paper would become absolutely saturated. And they had to be airtight so the cheese wouldn't rattle. It was all pure tin and we must have sold anything up to a hundred on a Monday morning. Kept our tinsmith going.

Another thing he used to make was the old cider mullers like they used to use in Father's pub. Father sold any amount of scrumpy and a lot of the men used to warm the stuff in these conical things which they'd put in the coal fire to heat, mulling the cider. It was a tin thing that tapered down to nothing on the end of a handle. Some of the cider drinkers would take a red hot poker and stick in it. We made them for Sam Durbin's pub in Cheddar. My tinsmith lived in Axbridge, two or three miles away, and he'd walk to work at my shop and be there at seven in the morning and wouldn't leave till six at night. All for about £3 a week. Oh, you'll get me going on all day, going back over all these years!"

"Ah, the sheep dip. The remains of that old dipping place are still down there today — the stones and that. What they had was a bayed-up pool in the river where t'was deep enough for them to throw the sheep in to clean them off before they were shorn. Once the creature had been thrown in one of the men would hold its head above water with a long crook on a pole, while someone else would give it a good scrubbing with a big broomstick thing to get out all the mud and muck from the fleece. Right by the side there was a bit of land, fenced off for the sheep to run and dry off, and they'd stay there till they were driven off for shearin'. Chaps used to go from farm to farm doin' that, pitching their tents in the farmer's field while they did his sheep, and then movin' on next day to another lot for someone else. I used to watch all that in the summertime when I was a lad."

"I am one of the beautiful hills of Cheddar — Jim Hill! I started work when I was thirteen an' from that day on I looked after 100 odd sheep for nearly 60 years, an' took a hundred lambs up to Priddy Fair every year for 50 years. In those days you did start work at six in the mornin' — punctual — an' if you finished by six in the evenin' you were lucky. My first wages was four and sixpence, but I could go tuh Weston with three bob an' I were a millionaire.

We never had more than 100 ewes or so but by the time they'd had 150 or 160 lambs t'was close on 300. Durin' lambin' time I've been for a solid week an' hab'n took me clothes off. I'm not gonna tell you I hab'n bin to sleep, but I'd come in an' sit in the chair an' catch as catch can. Have a nap occasionally. That all happened in the first week in March. To start with we used to have Border Leicester ewes, a sheep that cannot stick the wet climate. Well, we had them down on the moors and they all died with the liver fluke. I used to have the horse and cart and go out every other day and haul away a load and throw them down a great hole. By the time I'd finished there were 100 of them down there.

Sometimes, when sheep are put on wet ground, their hooves do go all soft and rotten and then I did have to pare away the outside horn with my knife and put some Stockholm tar between their cloves. Then p'raps when a couple of rams had bin fightin', and hurt their heads, I'd put some of it on the sores and it'd preserve it an' heal it an' keep the flies off. I have heard it said that when folk do say, *'Don't spoil a ship for a ha'poth of tar',* it should be, *'Don't spoil a sheep',* 'cause all the Mendipers do call them 'ship' and that's how the saying originated. But, whether or not t'is true, I couldn't tell you.

Another thing I'll tell you about — the haymakin'. I've done the lot — the mowin', the collectin', pitchin' into the agrivator or up on the mow helpin'. T'is an elevator really, but we did call it the agrivator 'cause sometimes he'd go an' sometimes he 'ouldn'. When t'were all finished Joe Muggins here did do the thatchin' of the mow. An' I made the spars an' the stretchers to do it with. Bin out in the winter an' cut the briars that did hang down from the hedges — bring 'em home an' drag 'em through a chain to pull all the thorns off to make the stretchers. Then I'd make the spars to hold them down. I've even gone to the extent of makin' clothes pegs. I were a bit of a gipsy once.

If you ever offered to pay the men for haymakin' you'd insult them. You'd take 'em out a loaf an' a couple o' pound o' cheese an' give 'em the run of the cider barrel. They wouldn' know when they'd had enough an' they'd eat an' drink, an' eat an' drink, an' when t'were finished down they'd go. An' I'd hitch up the horse an' home they'd go. Got one chap home one night an' his wife were so cross she were gonna shoot me, an' I thought, right, the next chap as gets drunk can take hisself home. But they drank so much they didn' know if they belonged to therself or the Salvation Army. Drunk? They'd be blinal! We'd get them come down to the cowhouse fer the night, lyin' out in the slurry an' water an' everythin'. I've put a rope round their legs an' dragged them out through it an' they wouldn' know the difference.

I 'spect I were about fourteen when I fetched me fust load o' coal fer the farmer tuh use. Five or six of us used tuh go wie carts — start off from here at two in the mornin' an' go tuh Chilcompton or Farrington or Kilmersdon. If we went to Farrington we'd have to put on an extra horse — a trace horse — to come up Rush Hill, and because that hill was so steep we started goin' to Kilmersdon. That was probably a mile further but t'was a better road, not so steep, and t'was lovely coal. We used to get a couple or three ton. Tenpence ha'penny a hundredweight. With all that weight on we had to put drug shoes under the wheels comin' down the Gorge. You can only drag a wheel so far on the brake 'cause the metal tyre gets so hot you burst the bond, so we either had the drug shoes or we'd have loaded drays draggin' behind. They'd be loaded down wie coal or rocks or swedes — whatever you were haulin' —

and that did help hold the waggon back."

"Can I interrupt a minute, 'cause this is interesting. My father was once talking to an old chap, who lived up in the Lippiatt, who reckoned his place was haunted and he wanted Father to go up and hear it for himself. T'wasn't every day, but most days. Well, Father went up and was having a cup of tea in front of an old fashioned range when suddenly the old fellow said, "Hark", and Father could definitely hear horses' hooves coming from behind the grate. Father thought it queer and couldn't understand it but said it wasn't a haunting. Then it suddenly came to him — the coal carts used to come over the Mendips taking the stuff to the local merchants and Cheddar station, and when they got to the Wind Rock they'd put the

The Lippiatt.

drug shoes on and the horses would stamp their hooves down hard. He checked the times out and there it was! The noises stopped once the carts got down. So it proved that a honeycombe of passages linked right down through from the Gorge to the Lippiatt. Some years later that cottage belonged to me and we pulled the grate out and, lo and behold, there was a cavity behind it!"

"You finished, then? Anyhow, other times I did go up fer the ochre on Axbridge Hill. Watty Evans would go up with his waggon and drag it out to the road and I used to come out after and take it down to Church Street, to what they called the Ochre Works — where Church Farm is now. They used to dry it and grind it and analyse it and then t'was manufactured into paint. T'was a dull yellow mud affair, just like a malm. It was found in patches up there. You might go up and dig all day or all week and not find half an ounce and then go up next day and hit a pocket. I were haulin' from one pocket up there that were 80 foot deep — the best they ever had up there, lovely stuff. That were the hole what I put them sheep down. Oh, tons and tons of ochre I hauled down. Then I'd go to Ubley fer the red oxide — fetched several loads from there and hauled back, but that were more like rock — in blocks — not clayey stuff. They did grind that down there and I'd haul it to Cheddar station fer it to be sent off to Matlock, in Derby, fer it tuh be processed.

Once a year we used the farm carts tuh take the children tuh Weston. We'd have this outin' fer all the children in Cheddar an' all the farmers in the village would take them. Maybe twenty carts would go, some of 'em were spring carts, an' the children would have tuh get out goin' up Banwell Hill, 'cause t'was too much for the horse. An' what was I like as a kid? A little ragged-ass devil. We'll say a street-urchin. Didn' give a cuss fer anybody. We young 'uns used tuh walk up the cliffs every night to what we call the Horseshoe Bend — just afore you come to the steepest part the Gorge. We'd loiter about an' bide there fer a bit an' then come back down tuh the Market Cross, just talkin' an' wand'rin' about. Never wen' in the caves though, neither of 'em. I were born an' bred in Cheddar an' could go in there fer nothin', but I never did. I don' take any more int'rest in them than if they wadd'n there. Amazin'.

As we got older we did go further afield, go up Cookham Hill an' p'raps meet a gang of Shipham blokes to have a fight. They'd reckon we were comin' up after their girls an' hadn' any right to. We'd get in a fight near enough every month. But t'waddn' nothin' serious. Just a word 'n' a blow. An' the ladies nowadays? Well, I'm a bachelor an' I'll make no comment an' then I shan't get into no hot water. An' as fer whether I should have bin a diplomat, well, yes and no. So now then, what does I think of Cheddar today? Well, t'is definitely growin'. More highly populated. I think there's a lot of rogues in Cheddar an' a lot of gentlemen. But, you know, we used to cut some capers in the old days. Compared with years ago t'is more classified now, but we were more happier — more contented all those years ago than what we are today. Thass my version."

Entrance to
Cheddar Cliffs

el **placer** de **LEER** CON **SUSAETA**

La Primera Guerra Mundial

Temas históricos

Textos de Erica Carracedo
Ilustraciones de Toni Rodríguez

PAÍSES MÁS IMPLICADOS

Imperio austrohúngaro

Comprendía más de diez nacionalidades: austriacos, húngaros, checos, eslovacos, polacos, rumanos, italianos, croatas, bosnios, serbios, eslovenos…, pero solo los dos primeros tenían poder.

Imperio ruso

Ocupaba los actuales territorios de Rusia, Bielorrusia, parte de Polonia, el Cáucaso, Finlandia, la mayor parte de Asia central y un trozo de Turquía.

Imperio alemán

Desde 1871, estaba compuesto por cuatro reinos (Prusia, Baviera, Wurtemberg y Sajonia), las provincias de Alsacia y Lorena y numerosos ducados.

Imperio británico

Era el imperio más extenso ya que, gracias a sus colonias, ocupaba territorios de los cinco continentes: África, Asia, América, Europa y Oceanía.

Francia

Después del Imperio británico, era el país con más colonias, ya que dominaba el centro y norte de África y también el sudeste asiático (Indochina).

Italia

Sufrió una dura unificación territorial (1848-1871) que imposibilitó su colonialismo. Permanece neutral en la Gran Guerra hasta 1915.

Imperio otomano

Desde finales del siglo XIX fue perdiendo poco a poco sus territorios hasta reducirse a la actual Turquía. En noviembre de 1914 se convierte en aliado de Alemania.

Estados Unidos

Su expansionismo fue escaso por América y el Pacífico, pero vital desde el punto de vista estratégico. Hasta 1917 no entra en la Primera Guerra Mundial.

Índice

¿Cómo empezó la I Guerra Mundial?

Nadie podía imaginar que el asesinato del heredero al trono del Imperio austrohúngaro a manos de un nacionalista serbio en la ciudad de Sarajevo fuese a desencadenar la Primera Guerra Mundial, que tanta muerte y destrucción trajo consigo.

La Gran Guerra, nombre que recibió en su época la Primera Guerra Mundial, duró cuatro años, desde 1914 hasta 1918, y participaron en ella 32 países de los cinco continentes, por eso se considera mundial.

En aquellos momentos, existía una Europa enfrentada por asuntos coloniales, comerciales o territoriales; así que los gobiernos de los distintos países creían ver en la guerra la solución inmediata a sus problemas.

Pronto lamentarían las terribles consecuencias, puesto que perdieron la vida casi 10 millones de soldados y 20 millones resultaron heridos.

El asesinato que cambió el mundo

El hecho concreto que desencadenó el conflicto fue el asesinato a tiros, el 28 de junio de 1914, del archiduque Francisco Fernando de Austria y su mujer durante su visita oficial a Sarajevo, capital de Bosnia, que desde 1908 era una provincia del Imperio austrohúngaro, arrebatada al Imperio otomano (los turcos).

El asesino era un estudiante serbio del grupo nacionalista *Mano Negra*. Este grupo luchaba por separar Bosnia del Imperio austriaco y crear una Gran Serbia.

Austria-Hungría responsabilizó a Serbia de fomentar este crimen y aprovechó la ocasión para lanzarle un ultimátum con condiciones durísimas para los serbios. El Imperio ruso acudió en defensa de Serbia debido a los intereses que tenía en los Balcanes, mientras que el Imperio alemán apoyó al austrohúngaro. Quedaron así rotas las relaciones diplomáticas.

Localización de Bosnia y Serbia en los Balcanes

Los grandes imperios coloniales a finales del siglo XIX

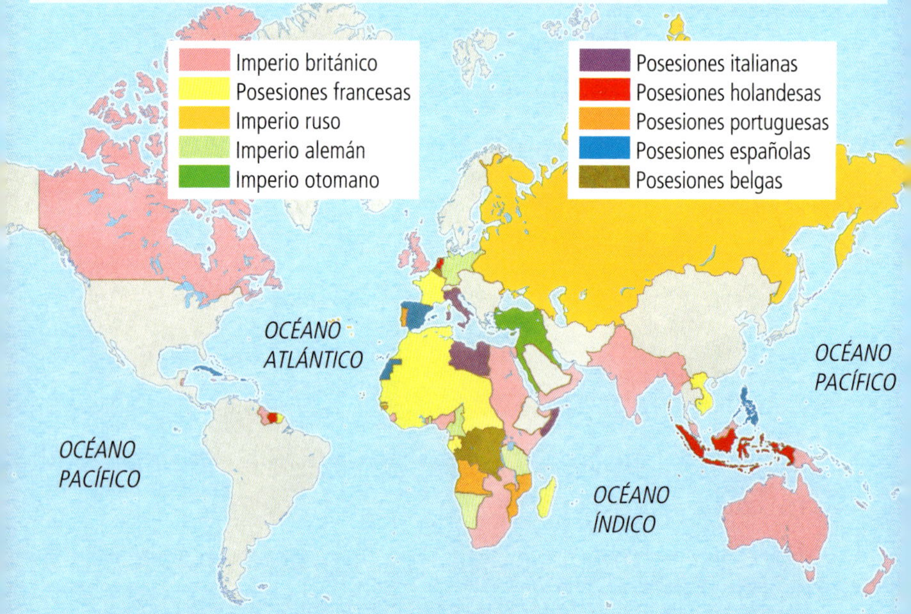

Causas reales de la I Guerra Mundial

Las causas profundas del enfrentamiento hay que buscarlas mucho antes, a finales del siglo XIX. Gran Bretaña (entonces Imperio británico), Francia y Alemania (entonces Imperio alemán) se habían convertido en países muy industrializados, pero solo los dos primeros poseían extensas colonias en Asia y África; así que Alemania se sentía en desventaja.

La carrera de armamentos

¡A ver quién tiene más armas!

Antes de estallar la guerra, todos los países habían comenzado una carrera contra reloj para armarse. Los mandos militares querían poseer más y mejores armas que sus rivales.

Alemania superaba a Gran Bretaña en el sector industrial gracias a las empresas mineras e industriales concentradas en la cuenca del Rhur. Fabricó ingentes cantidades de artillería (cañones, ametralladoras, fusiles, acorazados, etc.) que fueron almacenadas hasta el inicio de la guerra.

Sin embargo, Francia y Gran Bretaña poseían inmensos territorios coloniales, capaces de aportar inagotables cantidades de materias primas y combatientes.

En cuanto al potencial marítimo, la flota de Gran Bretaña superaba en cantidad a la alemana, pero Alemania la aventajaba con un ejército perfectamente entrenado y equipado.

Además había rivalidades de tipo territorial. Por un lado, Francia y Alemania se disputaban las regiones fronterizas de Alsacia y Lorena y, por otro, el Imperio ruso y el Imperio austrohúngaro estaban interesados en los Balcanes.

¿Qué eran los Balcanes? Esta península del sureste de Europa conformaba un puzle de gentes de distintas lenguas, religiones, etnias, tradiciones... y eran habituales los choques nacionalistas, pues había serbios, bosnios, rumanos, checos, eslovacos, croatas, etc.

Rivalidades territoriales en Europa

Durante siglos, los turcos habían dominado la zona, pero a finales del siglo XIX la debilidad de su imperio fue aprovechada por varias fuerzas políticas:

- Serbia consigue la independencia en 1875 y pretende liderar el movimiento de unificación de los pueblos eslavos.
- El Imperio austrohúngaro se anexiona Bosnia en 1908.
- Rusia, que se consideraba la protectora de los pueblos eslavos, quiere dominar el estrecho de los Dardanelos pese a la oposición británica.

Dirigentes políticos de la época

¿Quiénes declararon la guerra?

Francisco José I
Imperio austrohúngaro

Este emperador provocó tensiones nacionalistas al anexionar Bosnia. Muerto su hijo varón, su heredero era su sobrino, el archiduque asesinado.

Guillermo II
Imperio alemán

Fue el último káiser (emperador) alemán. Su afán expansionista le movió a construir una gran flota naval que pudiera competir con la de Gran Bretaña.

Nicolás II
Imperio ruso

Fue el último zar (jefe político y religioso) de Rusia y primo de Jorge V y Guillermo II. Contra su poder autoritario se hizo la revolución de 1917, que le obligó a abdicar.

Raymond Poincaré
República francesa

Presidente de Francia que antes de estallar la guerra había facilitado la alianza con Rusia, promoviendo inversiones francesas en ese país.

Víctor Manuel III
Reino de Italia

Para aumentar el territorio nacional, este rey provocó la guerra contra los turcos en 1911-1912 y entró en 1915 en la I Guerra Mundial.

Jorge V
Imperio británico

Aunque estaba emparentado con Guillermo II, fueron adversarios debido a las ansias alemanas de convertirse en potencia mundial.

Estalla la Gran Guerra

El Imperio austrohúngaro responsabilizó a Serbia del asesinato del heredero y, un mes después, le declaró la guerra. Acto seguido, Rusia movilizó sus tropas para defenderla.

El 1 de agosto Alemania entró en guerra con Rusia y los días siguientes se sumaron otros países al conflicto bélico, formando dos bloques enfrentados:

- Francia, Rusia y Gran Bretaña, llamadas las potencias aliadas o «los aliados». A ellos se sumaron Serbia y Bélgica al ser atacadas y, posteriormente, Italia (1915), Rumanía (1916), Grecia (1917) y Estados Unidos (1917). En agosto de 1914 también reciben ayuda puntual de Japón.
- Alemania y el Imperio austrohúngaro, denominadas las potencias centrales, recibieron ayuda del Imperio otomano (1914) y de Bulgaria (1915).

En total, durante los cuatro años de guerra combatieron ¡más de 70 millones de soldados! Demasiado sufrimiento.

Países que intervinieron

Potencias aliadas

- Gran Bretaña y sus colonias
- Francia y sus colonias
- Imperio ruso
- Países aliados a ellas
- Incorporación tardía en el bando aliado

Potencias centrales

- Alemania y sus colonias
- Imperio austrohúngaro
- Países aliados a ellas

Países neutrales:

en la Gran Guerra

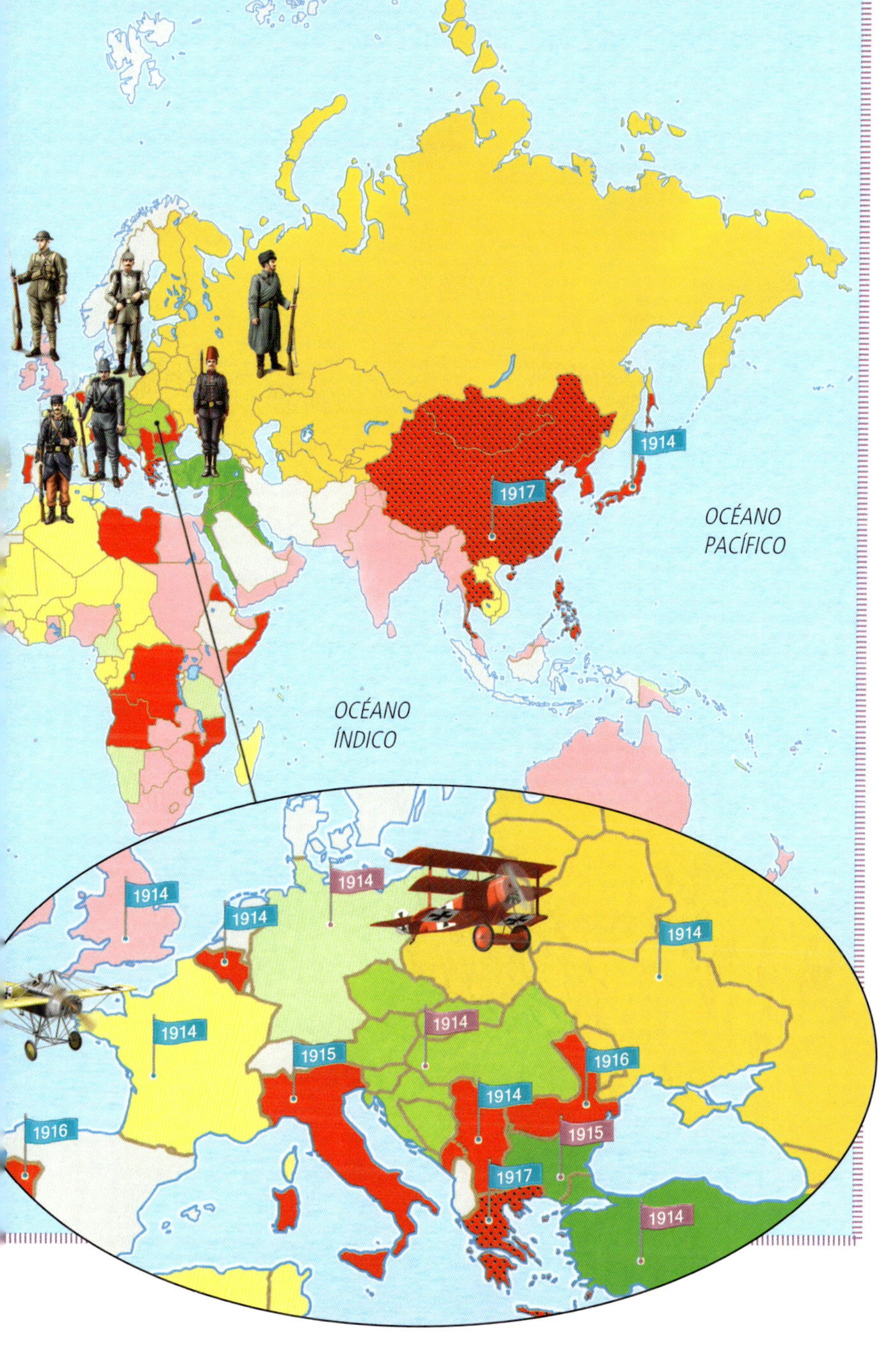

➪ Letrero: «Agencia de reclutamiento militar».

Avances terrestres y trincheras

Ambos bandos contaron con muchos voluntarios deseosos de ir al frente. Desde el primer momento, se formaron enormes filas de jóvenes entusiasmados por alistarse y luchar por su patria. Pensaban que sería una guerra corta, pero el tiempo les hizo ver lo equivocados que estaban. Pronto se dieron cuenta de que «no estarían en casa por Navidad».

Fase 1: guerra de movimientos

La primera fase de la contienda, de agosto a noviembre de 1914, se basó en el movimiento continuo de los soldados en ofensivas y contraofensivas.

Como fuerza de combate se usó la infantería, es decir, el avance a pie de los soldados. Sus armas fundamentales en esta lucha cuerpo a cuerpo eran las bayonetas. ¿En qué consistían estas armas? Sencillamente, eran rifles a los que se acoplaba un cuchillo en el cañón.

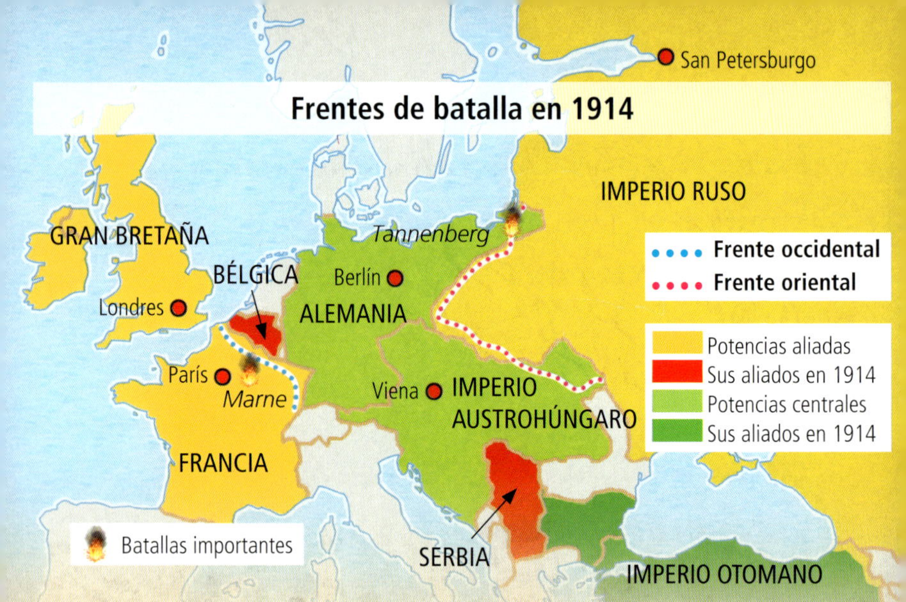

Al comienzo de la guerra se abrieron dos frentes de batalla: el frente occidental (entre Alemania y el norte de Francia) y el frente oriental (entre Alemania y Rusia), con lo cual Alemania tenía dos enemigos, uno por la derecha (Rusia) y otro por la izquierda (Francia).

¿Qué plan ideó Alemania ante esta situación? El ejército alemán se dirigió primero hacia Francia, pensando que sería una campaña rápida, para luego centrarse en su enfrentamiento con Rusia.

De camino a Francia, ocupó Bélgica, que hasta el momento era un país neutral.

Mientras los belgas resistían, Gran Bretaña desplazaba sus tropas por el norte de dicho país para acudir en su ayuda.

La batalla más importante se dio en torno al río Marne, un afluente del Sena justo al este de París. Unos 500 taxis parisinos transportaron a 4.000 soldados al frente. Resultado: los alemanes no pudieron llegar a la capital francesa.

A este fracaso se sumó que los rusos avanzaban en el frente oriental, así que Alemania mandó refuerzos allí y logró vencer en agosto en la batalla de Tannenberg.

Los animales en la guerra

¡Usos verdaderamente sorprendentes!

Aunque en la batalla del Marne se transportó a los combatientes por medio de taxis, lo habitual era el uso del tren o de miles de caballos que fueron reclutados de granja en granja durante los días previos al conflicto.

Los animales siempre han sido de vital importancia en las contiendas y su utilización fue muy diversa en esta guerra.

Palomas mensajeras

Los generales las usaron para dar órdenes a sus tropas situadas en el campo de batalla. Las palomas no sufrían interferencias, como ocurría con los sistemas de telecomunicaciones. Resultaban ideales por su formidable instinto de orientación y su resistencia a la fatiga y a los cambios climáticos.

Fotógrafas ocasionales

En 1907 se inventó una cámara fotográfica que se ajustaba a las palomas y así podían dar una visión del terreno desde las alturas; pero el gran desarrollo de la aviación descartó rápidamente su uso.

Perros multiusos

Nuestros inseparables amigos los perros fueron mensajeros, vigías durante la noche, animales de tiro que transportaban cañones y heridos, y también fieles mascotas.

Canarios para los gases

Cuando se excavaban túneles profundos en las trincheras, podían liberarse los gases acumulados bajo tierra. Por eso, la muerte repentina de los canarios dentro de una galería avisaba a los soldados de la presencia de estos gases tóxicos.

Fase 2: guerra de trincheras

En otoño de 1914 los dos bandos cambian de estrategia en el frente occidental. En lugar de avanzar con tropas en el campo de batalla, se inicia el choque frontal de soldados desde sus trincheras. Comienza así la segunda fase, que duró de noviembre de 1914 a finales de 1916.

Las trincheras eran cientos de kilómetros de zanjas excavadas en la tierra, donde los soldados quedaban protegidos de las

trinchera alemana

ametralladoras de los adversarios. Tras bombardear a la línea enemiga, los soldados salían a enfrentarse cuerpo a cuerpo.

La vida en la trinchera no era nada fácil. Además de sufrir los bombardeos, estos jóvenes convivían con el frío y la humedad del largo invierno, el barro, la mala alimentación, la proliferación de ratas y piojos, la falta de higiene, la incomodidad y el miedo a la proximidad del enemigo, que acechaba a pocos metros.

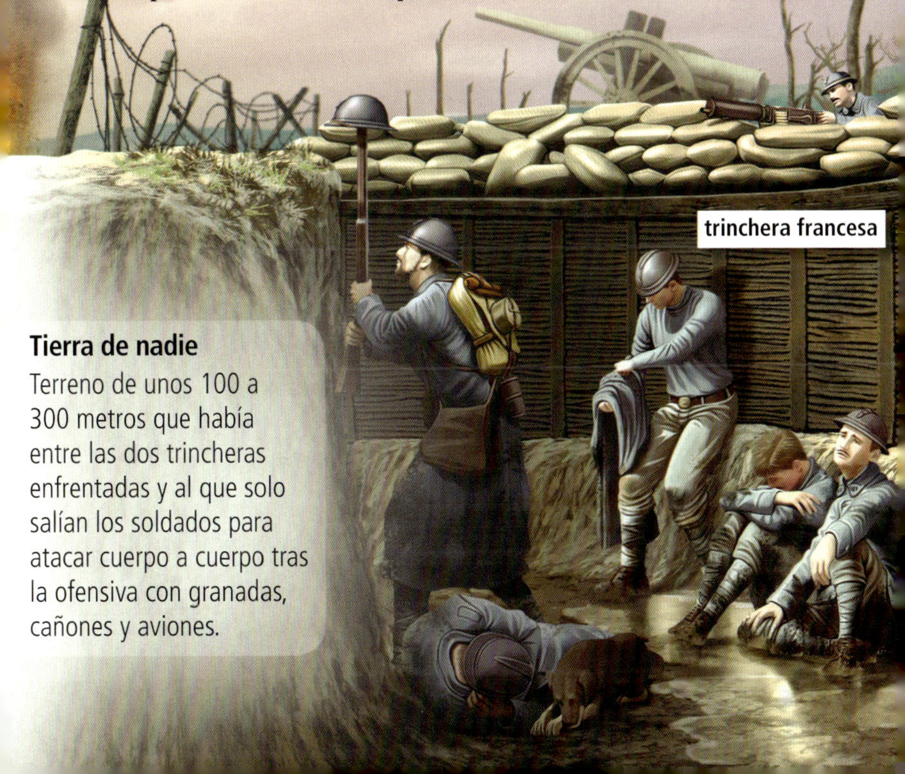

Tierra de nadie
Terreno de unos 100 a 300 metros que había entre las dos trincheras enfrentadas y al que solo salían los soldados para atacar cuerpo a cuerpo tras la ofensiva con granadas, cañones y aviones.

Cartas de amor desde el frente

Ma chérie… Meine liebe…

Mientras los altos mandos se comunicaban con sus tropas por medio de palomas mensajeras, telégrafos y teléfonos de campaña, que llenaban de cables los suelos de las trincheras, los soldados mandaban cartas a sus familias.

Existía un sistema eficaz de correos que permitía hacer llegar las cartas en un plazo no muy largo de tiempo.

Los soldados contaban aspectos cotidianos de la vida en el frente, pero si en las cartas aparecían frases desalentadoras o se daban detalles de las operaciones militares, se confiscaban y nunca llegaban a su destino.

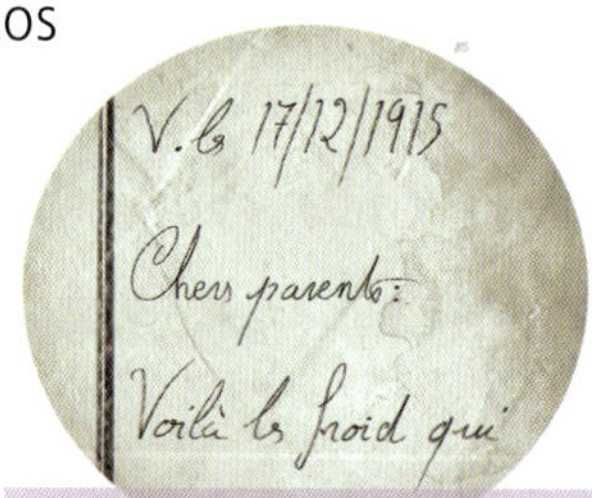

⇨ Carta: «Verdún, 17-12-1915
Queridos padres: Por aquí el frío…».

➪ Pancartas: «¡Abajo los monopolios de alimentos!». «¡La leche infantil no se toca!».

En 1916, ambos bloques ven que el conflicto se alarga y no hay ganadores ni vencidos. Los frentes de la guerra apenas se han movido. Será en este momento cuando se fabriquen nuevas armas más mortíferas para romper ese equilibrio.

En las ciudades, se inician las primeras movilizaciones pacifistas de una población harta de la subida de precios de productos básicos y de tener a sus hombres lejos de casa sufriendo las penurias de la guerra.

¡Ataques desde el cielo!

Antes de esta guerra, los enfrentamientos bélicos se realizaban entre ejércitos que combatían entre sí sin afectar a la población civil. Por eso en 1915 los ciudadanos de Londres no supieron reaccionar cuando unos zepelines (globos dirigibles) aparecieron por sorpresa en el cielo. Al caer las primeras bombas entendieron que lo mejor era ponerse a cubierto. Mujeres,

ancianos y niños sufrieron aterrorizados los bombardeos, que se repitieron en otras ciudades inglesas y francesas.

Los zepelines eran artefactos muy lentos y además peligrosos para sus tripulantes, pues, al estar llenos de gas, podían explotar fácilmente si los alcanzaban con munición incendiaria. Por ello se usaron de manera esporádica y casi al final de la contienda se sustituyeron por los bombarderos *Gotha*, que alcanzaban los 100 km/hora y podían volar 5 o 6 horas sin repostar debido a su mayor carga de combustible.

Las nuevas armas de guerra

El lado oscuro del avance tecnológico

La Revolución Industrial del siglo XIX favoreció el invento de armas que se usaron en tierra, mar y aire. Había que romper el estancamiento en la fase de trincheras, y surgieron instrumentos de ataque más mortíferos para provocar el desempate.

Tanque (vehículo acorazado)

Este invento inglés atravesaba las alambradas de espino de las trincheras sin dificultad. Sin embargo, eran muy lentos (6 km/h) y no se agarraban bien al terreno embarrado, por lo que podían incluso volcar.

Ametralladora

El perfeccionamiento de esta arma permitió matar a distancia y de forma masiva, pues disparaba unas 400 balas por minuto. Su peso, que oscilaba entre 15 y 50 kg, obligaba a los soldados a arrastrarse con ellas por el suelo o a apoyarlas en las trincheras.

Aeroplanos

Al principio servían para espiar desde el aire, pero pronto se convierten en armas mortíferas. Había varios tipos: monoplano, biplano y triplano, según el número de planos del ala. A mayor número se conseguía más resistencia y maniobrabilidad, pero menos velocidad.

Artillería: cañones y obuses

Mientras que el cañón disparaba un proyectil hacia objetivos visibles, el obús lanzaba granadas más pesadas con un tiro curvo y alto hacia un blanco no apreciado a simple vista, por lo que la ayuda aérea era fundamental para corregir los errores de dirección. Su manejo necesitaba de 4 a 6 soldados y era preciso un terreno liso para asentar bien la estructura.

Gases venenosos

Los alemanes son los primeros en desarrollarlos, pero enseguida los aliados los copiarán. Ante los primeros ataques con gas, los soldados solo pudieron taparse la nariz con su propia ropa; después se fabricaron máscaras antigás para humanos y animales.

Minas: terrestres y marinas

En secreto, se excavaba la tierra hasta llegar a la trinchera enemiga y se hacía detonar las minas. A veces, estallaban antes de tiempo y alertaban de la intención del adversario. En el mar, las minas ayudaron a bloquear el paso de los barcos comerciales que transportaban material de guerra.

El desarrollo de la aviación

En un principio, los aeroplanos tenían la función de vigilar al contrario y, una vez en tierra, facilitar fotos e informes sobre la posición de los puestos de mando, las rutas por las que recibían los suministros y las instrucciones para que la artillería acertara en el blanco la próxima vez que disparara.

El siguiente paso consistió en dotar de ametralladoras a estos aeroplanos para que atacasen a otros aviones enemigos en el aire. Nacían así los primeros *cazas*.

El problema radicaba en dónde situar las ametralladoras para que el piloto pudiera agarrar los mandos y, a la vez, apuntar al objetivo, y todo ello sin que los disparos frontales dañaran las hélices. La primera medida fue forrarlas con placas de metal para que las balas rebotaran. Después se ideó un sistema que detectaba si el aspa coincidía en la trayectoria de la munición y, de ser así, paraba el lanzamiento de la carga para no dañar esa parte esencial del avión.

El terror del aire: el Barón Rojo

La leyenda de un héroe alemán

Manfred von Richthofen, más conocido como el *Barón Rojo,* fue el encargado de dirigir con su triplano rojo, de ahí su apodo, un escuadrón de 14 aeroplanos que ocasionaron el pánico en el abril sangriento de 1917. Se les llamaba «el circo volante» porque cada avión de estos escuadrones estaba pintado de un vivo color y se movían itinerantes por el frente occidental. Con el ataque en grupo, Alemania compensaba así su escaso número de aviones frente a la Fuerza Aérea Británica.

Como tantos otros aviadores, el Barón Rojo empezó en la caballería, pero al quedar esta prácticamente anulada por el uso de bombas y alambradas en las trincheras, decidió que su sitio estaba en la emocionante aviación.

Tuvo el triste récord de haber derribado más de 80 aviones. Murió con 25 años en pleno vuelo.

¿Cómo era la vida de los pilotos?

Estos jóvenes aviadores tenían dos peligros: el enemigo que buscaba su derribo y el caprichoso tiempo atmosférico. En las alturas, los pilotos pasaban muchísimo frío, tanto que el sudor y el orín se les congelaban, y notaban la falta de oxígeno. Pero cuando aterrizaban la cosa cambiaba, pues podían asearse y dormir tranquilos, no como la desdichada infantería de las trincheras. Claro que no todos volvían, pues muchos morían en los enfrentamientos aéreos.

Pero esto no provocaba un ambiente de tristeza en el aeródromo, sino todo lo contrario: se extendía el sentimiento de disfrute de la vida y, una vez acabada la jornada, los afortunados aviadores celebraban sus hazañas en la cantina, donde exponían sus trofeos arrancados de los aparatos derribados, tales como trozos de hélices, de ametralladoras o la propia numeración del avión.

La guerra en el mar

Las dos grandes potencias marítimas, Gran Bretaña y Alemania, sabían lo importante que era para el final de la guerra el bloqueo del oponente en el mar. Las materias primas no llegarían a las fábricas, los alimentos escasearían en las ciudades y trincheras, y los soldados no podrían avanzar.

Antes de iniciar la contienda, Alemania, consciente de la superioridad naval británica, intentó igualar su flota construyendo enormes buques de guerra.

Al no conseguirlo, optó por el uso de submarinos o barcos sumergibles, con fines militares, lo que supuso una gran novedad.

En febrero de 1915, los submarinos alemanes comenzaron a atacar a los mercantes que se acercaban a Gran Bretaña y Francia. Enfrentarse a buques de guerra se consideraba juego limpio, pero hundir barcos comerciales desarmados, no.

Las normas de navegación exigían registrar el navío en busca de material bélico. Si lo

encontraban, debía ser escoltado a puerto para confiscar su carga o destruirlo, pero salvando la vida de sus tripulantes. Con un submarino no se podía hacer eso, porque si emergía perdía el efecto sorpresa del ataque. Además, no tenía la potencia para arrastrar un barco a puerto y tampoco contaba con espacio para los pasajeros del buque. Así pues, hundían los barcos con la carga y los marineros a bordo.

Más cruel fue todavía cuando en mayo de 1915 un submarino hundió un lujoso crucero británico cerca de Irlanda: el *Lusitania*. Murieron más de 1.200 personas, entre ellas 100 americanos, lo que provocó que EEUU empezara a plantearse la entrada en la guerra, aunque aún esperó hasta 1917.

¿Cómo se malvivía en un submarino?

Los marineros a bordo de estos barcos sumergibles no tenían comodidades. El agua fresca y los alimentos escaseaban, y no podían lavarse con asiduidad.

El submarino alemán

Un enemigo invisible

El ingeniero español Jerónimo de Ayanz y Beaumont no podía imaginarse en el siglo XVII que su invento, un sumergible para observaciones subacuáticas, iba a alcanzar un impacto tan significativo en la Gran Guerra.

Desde su creación fue perfeccionándose para viajar largas distancias bajo el agua, pero ahora el objetivo era torpedear barcos por sorpresa. Así, el submarino torpedero, inventado en 1888 por el también español Isaac Peral, será utilizado en la I Guerra Mundial para atacar tanto acorazados como barcos comerciales, sin importar si pertenecían a países beligerantes o neutrales en este conflicto bélico.

Se proporcionó más autonomía a sus tanques de combustible, lo cual evitaba subir a la superficie para repostar; se aumentó el número de torpedos que podía disparar y se le incorporó una radio para comunicarse con otros buques.

La temperatura en el interior era de 30 °C y el olor, una mezcla de aceites, caucho, pintura y el propio de los tripulantes, que se aseaban muy poco. ¡Era insoportable!

Dentro de los submarinos había muchos peligros, como las inundaciones, las colisiones con rocas bajo el mar o la asfixia de los hombres debido al monóxido de carbono (gas mortífero producido por el motor de petróleo). Para alertar de su presencia, los ratones fueron fundamentales, pues estos animalitos detectaban la falta de oxígeno antes que los humanos.

¡Las flotas salen de puerto!

Durante meses, tanto la Marina Real británica como la Flota de Alta Mar alemana permanecieron resguardadas en sus respectivos puertos eludiendo el choque frontal. Esto se debía a la inferioridad numérica de los buques de guerra o *acorazados* de Alemania y al escaso deseo de todos los altos mandos de arriesgarse a perder unos navíos carísimos e insustituibles. Pero en febrero de 1916, Scheer, el nuevo almirante alemán, más decidido que su antecesor, propuso hacer algunas incursiones en el mar del Norte.

Diario de una batalla: Jutlandia

El cazador es cazado

En la tarde del 31 de mayo de 1916, las flotas británica y alemana se encontraron cerca de la península de Jutlandia (Dinamarca) en una batalla naval que duró dos días.

El plan alemán

El almirante Scheer quería ir hundiendo por partes la Marina Real británica, pues era consciente de la superioridad de esta. Lanzaría al mar los barcos de Hipper y así atraería al almirante inglés Beatty hacia el resto de la Flota de Alta Mar alemana antes de que el inglés Jellicoe llegara en su auxilio. Pero los ingleses se enteraron de sus intenciones descifrando las transmisiones alemanas y toda la Marina Real salió a su encuentro.

Encuentro inesperado

En alta mar ninguno conocía la posición del enemigo, por lo que se desplegaron en busca de las naves del adversario. Inesperadamente, los cruceros de combate de Beatty se encontraron con los de Hipper. Varios errores hicieron que Beatty fuera un blanco fácil: se colocó contra el horizonte, siendo así más visible su silueta, y sus cañones mal dirigidos tardaron en presentar batalla.

¡Rodeados!

Scheer llegó a la zona y Beatty aguantó en espera de Jellicoe. Al llegar el resto de la Marina Real británica, los alemanes quedaron rodeados y finalmente emprendieron la huida ante la superioridad numérica, aprovechando la oscuridad de la noche.

El desastroso resultado

Los británicos perdieron 14 barcos, con 6.100 bajas, y los alemanes 11, con 2.500 marineros. Técnicamente no hubo un vencedor pero los alemanes, al tener menos pérdidas, se consideraron los triunfadores, a pesar de que fueron los primeros en retirarse. De todas formas, ante tal desastre, las flotas de ambos países se volvieron a encerrar en sus puertos y Alemania potenció todavía más el uso de sus submarinos.

¿Cómo acabó? Vencedores y vencidos

En el frente oriental, el debilitado ejército ruso es incapaz de resistir y va replegándose ante los avances de las potencias centrales a principios de 1917.

En Petrogrado (principal área industrial de Rusia, hoy San Petersburgo) se dan numerosas protestas obreras y manifestaciones de mujeres, hartas de hacer colas para recoger los alimentos. Esta

situación se intensifica hasta convertirse en revueltas, que el zar Nicolás II intenta reprimir con crueldad. Los soldados, descontentos también, no cumplen las órdenes de disparar a los manifestantes y se unen a las protestas.

Finalmente, el zar tendrá que abdicar y se implanta un gobierno provisional que quiere proseguir con la impopular guerra. En octubre, el partido bolchevique, con Lenin a la cabeza, da un golpe de estado y por fin se pacta una salida de la guerra con Alemania a través de la firma del Tratado de Brest-Litovsk en 1918.

➪ Pancarta: «Necesitamos comida para nuestros niños y soldados».

Situación del frente occidental

La fase de trincheras finalizó en 1916 sin avances significativos y con miles de muertos en las batallas más largas de la guerra: Somme y Verdún, ambas en territorio francés.

Los alemanes se enfrentaban al tercer invierno de la guerra desmoralizados y desnutridos. Ante la falta de patatas por una mala cosecha se tuvieron que alimentar con nabos, de menor aporte energético. Por tanto, los motines y las deserciones estaban a la orden del día.

Propaganda de guerra

El inicio de la manipulación

La propaganda se convirtió por primera vez en una verdadera arma de guerra que alimentaba el odio al enemigo y mantenía la moral de los fatigados soldados.

Los aliados diseñaron la suya con mucha más eficacia que los alemanes, pues estos últimos pensaban que su Estado autoritario no necesitaba una movilización de su población, acostumbrada a seguir siempre las normas.

➪ Cartel: «Tu país te necesita».

Los mensajes de los carteles o las octavillas estaban destinados a encontrar voluntarios para el ejército, recaudar dinero para la guerra apelando al espíritu de sacrificio del pueblo y ridiculizar al oponente exagerando su maldad en la lucha.

No fue sino hasta el final del conflicto cuando los ciudadanos europeos descubrieron la magnitud de la manipulación de la que habían sido víctimas.

¡Por fin vienen los americanos!

Lo que no consiguió el hundimiento del *Lusitania* lo logró el telegrama del ministro de exteriores alemán, Zimmermann, enviado al embajador de México en enero de 1917. En él le prometía la devolución de los territorios anexionados por EE UU si México entraba en la guerra de su lado.

Nada salió conforme al plan. El servicio de inteligencia británico interceptó el mensaje, México no aceptó, pero la Fuerza Expedicionaria Americana amarraba en un puerto francés en junio, en ayuda de los aliados. Eran hombres corpulentos y bien alimentados, no como los agotados alemanes y austrohúngaros.

1918: el último intento alemán

Alemania intenta una ofensiva en marzo de 1918, pero los franceses e ingleses son ayudados por los estadounidenses. Consciente de la superioridad aliada, el bando alemán tendrá que retirarse en agosto de manera ordenada a sus fronteras.

Así pues, el 11 del mes once, a las 11 de la mañana, cesaba el fuego después de cuatro años de enfrentamientos, tras la firma del armisticio en un vagón de tren en la ciudad francesa de Compiègne.

Cariño, ¡bienvenido a casa!

La incomprensión de la sociedad

A menudo, al volver a su ansiado hogar, los combatientes se encontraron con la incomprensión de sus familiares ante las dramáticas experiencias sufridas, que les habían dejado mutilados o con serios trastornos psicológicos. Los alegres muchachos que habían marchado al frente no eran los mismos que ahora llegaban a casa, ¡la guerra los había cambiado demasiado!

Trauma de guerra

Demasiados días oyendo las ametralladoras y viendo morir a los amigos, pensando que ellos serían los siguientes, ocasionó que muchos combatientes perdieran la razón. No podían conciliar el sueño y, si lo hacían, era entre continuas pesadillas donde revivían aquellos horrorosos días. Algunos hasta perdieron el habla.

Rostros desfigurados

Algunos soldados tenían la cara deformada por la metralla o por las graves infecciones de las heridas, pues aún no existía el antibiótico que las curara, y sufrieron el rechazo social porque la gente se asustaba al verlos. En Gran Bretaña se realizaron las primeras reconstrucciones faciales.

Miembros amputados

Muchos combatientes habían perdido parte de la pierna debido al llamado «pie de trinchera». Si los soldados pasaban demasiado tiempo en una trinchera llena de agua hasta las rodillas en esos gélidos inviernos, el resultado era la gangrena de esa zona y por tanto su amputación. Por eso el sector de las prótesis tuvo un gran desarrollo en la posguerra.

Ciegos por el gas

Los gases venenosos empleados por ambos bandos provocaban en algunas ocasiones la muerte y en otras, quemaduras y ceguera. Los soldados tuvieron que aprender de nuevo a realizar las tareas cotidianas en la más absoluta oscuridad.

Tratado de Versalles: una paz impuesta

Los países vencedores fueron firmando diversos tratados de paz con cada una de las naciones derrotadas, pero imponiendo sus condiciones sin darles derecho a voz.

El 28 de junio de 1919, coincidiendo con el aniversario del atentado del heredero austrohúngaro, le tocó el turno a Alemania. El lugar elegido fue la galería de los Espejos del Palacio de Versalles, en Francia, país que impuso las condiciones más duras por las graves pérdidas que había sufrido. El tratado firmado exigía a Alemania el completo desarme, la pérdida de territorios y colonias y el pago de reparaciones. El pueblo alemán lo vivió como una humillación.

En palabras del presidente de EE UU, W. Wilson, esta fue una «guerra para acabar con todas las guerras». Se equivocaba, pues el fracaso de estos acuerdos, quizás porque los vencidos no intervinieron en ellos, provocó que, tan solo veinte años después, estallara la Segunda Guerra Mundial.

Consecuencias de la I Guerra Mundial

Se ponía fin a un conflicto que había durado demasiado y dejaba tras de sí una estela de muerte y destrucción como nunca se había vivido en Europa. Ahora había que afrontar las horrorosas consecuencias de esta terrible guerra.

Se estima que murieron casi 10 millones de soldados y más del doble sufrieron

heridas muy graves. La mayoría de las víctimas fueron hombres jóvenes, por lo que en las ciudades y pueblos casi no había más que mujeres, niños y ancianos, y de ellos muchos fallecieron de hambre.

El mapa europeo se transformó

Desaparecieron los grandes imperios y surgieron países nuevos con fronteras artificiales, ya que no coincidían con las nacionalidades. El imperio alemán perdió Alsacia y Lorena, parte de Polonia y sus colonias en África. Del austrohúngaro nacieron nuevos países: Austria, Hungría, Checoslovaquia y Yugoslavia. El imperio ruso cedió Finlandia, Estonia, Letonia, Lituania y parte de Polonia, y el imperio otomano se redujo a Turquía.

Europa cedió la supremacía a EE UU, que se alzó como potencia mundial debido a su decisiva intervención final en el conflicto, aunque de corta duración (solo un año y medio de actuación estadounidense de los cuatro que duró).

Mapa de Europa tras la Primera Guerra Mundial

A propuesta del presidente de EE UU, W. Wilson, se creó un organismo internacional, la Sociedad de Naciones, con el objetivo de garantizar la paz en el futuro y el desarme generalizado. Desde su propio nacimiento en 1920 fue un fracaso, porque algunas potencias se quedaron al margen: EE UU (pues el Congreso estadounidense paralizó la iniciativa del presidente), la Unión de Repúblicas Socialistas Soviéticas (URSS, antigua Rusia) y los países vencidos, como Alemania.

¿Hubo participación española?

Neutralidades que ahogan

Desde inicios del siglo XX, España estaba considerada un país de segundo rango debido a su debilidad militar tras la pérdida de sus colonias en 1898. Ni su ejército ni su flota eran comparables a los de las potencias combatientes, y su industria tampoco había tenido un gran desarrollo.

El gobierno español, consciente de la llamada «crisis del 98», optó por la neutralidad. Sin embargo, España se convirtió en suministradora de productos industriales y agrarios a todos los países beligerantes. Mientras los dueños de las fábricas y de las tierras aprovechaban la situación y se enriquecían vendiendo sus productos, las clases humildes pasaban hambre porque no podían comprar los alimentos básicos, que habían subido de precio al escasear en el mercado.

Cambios en la sociedad

En toda Europa se acentuaron las diferencias entre ricos y pobres. Los fabricantes y mercaderes de armas se enriquecieron, pero los trabajadores se empobrecieron ante la subida de precios de productos básicos, como el pan.

Otra consecuencia de la guerra fue el descenso de la natalidad, ya que los hombres estaban en el frente. En contrapartida y por primera vez en la historia, las mujeres desempeñaron los oficios propios de los varones, que habían quedado vacantes al ir ellos a combatir.

El papel de las mujeres

Una nueva vida fuera del hogar

Antes de la guerra, las mujeres habían sido campesinas, criadas, enfermeras o maestras, además de amas de casa; pero ahora se incorporaban a todos los puestos laborales dejados por los hombres que se habían movilizado.

Con el fin de la guerra, se exigió a las mujeres que volvieran a las tareas domésticas, pero estas habían demostrado al mundo, y a ellas mismas, que podían elegir su futuro.

Diversidad de trabajos

Comenzaron a trabajar como maquinistas de tren o autobús, operarias en fábricas de artillería, en las minas, en los altos hornos, etc., y también en la sombra, como espías, recopilando información para el bando contrario. Ejemplo de ello fue la conocidísima Mata Hari, que tenía en el Hotel Ritz de Madrid su centro de operaciones.

Cambio en la vestimenta

Para ganar comodidad en el nuevo mundo laboral, empezaron a usar faldas con menos capas y más cortas, que dejaban a la vista los tobillos. También optaron por peinados a base de recogidos menos extravagantes que en el siglo anterior y más aptos para el trabajo.

Casadas o solteras

Los hombres solteros escaseaban, pues muchos habían muerto en el frente y, además, la nueva independencia económica que tenían las jóvenes que trabajaban fuera del hogar les permitía decidir si querían casarse o permanecer solteras.

➩ Cartel: «Voto para las mujeres».

Voto femenino

Antes de la guerra el sexo femenino era considerado débil e intelectualmente inferior, por lo cual no se las dejaba votar. Pero durante la guerra las mujeres demostraron su capacidad y se multiplicaron los movimientos para pedir el derecho al voto. En algunos países, como Gran Bretaña, Alemania, Estados Unidos y Rusia, lo consiguieron; en otros, como Francia, tuvieron que esperar hasta 1948.

Nueva vida social

Antes de la guerra era impensable que una mujer saliera sola a la calle y pudiera disfrutar del deporte, el baile o la vida social. En cambio, después del conflicto apareció un nuevo modelo de muchacha que estudiaba, trabajaba, viajaba y se divertía, empezando a compartir también espacios de ocio con el hombre.

EEUU, el banquero de Alemania

Tras la guerra, todo estaba destrozado: casas, campos de cultivo, puentes, carreteras, vías del tren, fábricas, etc. Los países necesitaban reconstruir sus ciudades y pueblos y pidieron dinero prestado a la nueva potencia mundial: EEUU, que, al haber intervenido menos tiempo en la guerra y no haberse combatido en su territorio, no había sufrido tantas pérdidas.

De esta manera, el país con más deudas fue la vencida Alemania, pues unido a su propio desastre material tuvo que pagar a los aliados mucho dinero en concepto de indemnizaciones de guerra.

En este ambiente de caos, Adolf Hitler, un excombatiente humillado con la derrota, se alzó como orador entre la descontenta masa alemana.

Y veinte años después, este hombre, ya asentado en el gobierno alemán, iniciaba la Segunda Guerra Mundial, más cruel todavía que la Primera.

La I Guerra Mundial en imágenes

Cañones franceses en acción

Alemanes vigilando al enemigo

La I Guerra Mundial fue la primera gran guerra fotográfica, pues además de los fotógrafos profesionales que trabajaban para los periódicos, muchísimos soldados de ambos bandos compraron cámaras de bolsillo y captaron en imágenes su vida y los horrores de la guerra.

Respirando fuera del submarino

Tropas coloniales en la trinchera

CONTEXTO HISTÓRICO

A comienzos del siglo XX, Europa era la dueña del mundo. Parecía que reinaba el bienestar gracias a la industrialización, pero las tensiones internacionales y las desigualdades económicas estaban ocultas.

Con la guerra, el continente europeo se sumió en el caos, sobre todo Rusia, donde había una enorme desigualdad social. La mayoría de la población eran campesinos muy pobres, y los escasos obreros malvivían con largas jornadas laborales. Todos ellos sometidos al poder del zar, que se imponía con su ejército y vivía rodeado de lujo. En 1917 hubo muchas manifestaciones y huelgas obreras, el ejército se negó a aplastarlas y el zar tuvo que abdicar. Las potencias occidentales no quisieron apoyar la revolución rusa ni dejarla crecer, aun a costa del avance alemán. En octubre, el partido bolchevique tomó el poder, sacó al país de la impopular guerra y abolió la propiedad de la tierra. El triunfo de la revolución rusa animó a otras revueltas en Europa y a crear partidos comunistas en varios países, si bien la represión fue brutal.

Al final de la guerra, apareció una potencia mundial al otro lado del océano: EEUU, que había sido el proveedor de los aliados y ahora proponía un nuevo modelo de vida con los «felices años veinte». Fue la década de los espectáculos, la alta costura, el jazz y el blues, el cine de Hollywood y el consumismo desmesurado de electrodomésticos y automóviles.

COLECCIÓN *LEER CON SUSAETA*

Nivel 1. Empiezo a *LEER*

1. Animales de la granja • 2. Fiesta de brujas • 3. Castillos de miedo
4. Historias de ogros • 5. Historias de ponis
6. El porqué de los animales • 7. El porqué del cuerpo humano
8. Adivina adivinanza • 9. Caperucita Roja • 10. Pulgarcito
11. La bella durmiente • 12. Los tres cerditos
13. Fábulas de animales • 14. Historias de Hadas y Princesas
15. El mago de Oz • 16. Historias del Arca de Noé
17. Animales viajeros • 18. El mundo de los osos

Nivel 2. Ya sé *LEER*

1. Historias de dragones • 2. Caballeros medievales
3. El libro de la selva • 4. Pinocho • 5. La sirenita
6. Las princesas bailarinas • 7. La Bella y la Bestia • 8. Blancanieves
9. Cuentos españoles • 10. El Cid Campeador
11. El mundo de los tiburones • 12. Los mejores chistes
13. El mundo de los dinosaurios • 14. Historias de aviones
15. Nuestros amigos los perros • 16. Historias de barcos
17. Historias de trenes

Nivel 3. La aventura de *LEER*

1. La isla del tesoro • 2. El lazarillo de Tormes
3. Las aventuras de Tom Sawyer • 4. Mujercitas • 5. Sandokán
6. La vuelta al mundo en 80 días • 7. Un capitán de quince años
8. La cabaña del tío Tom • 9. La isla misteriosa • 10. Moby Dick
11. Robin Hood • 12. El prisionero de Zenda • 13. Los tres mosqueteros
14. Alicia en el país de las maravillas • 15. Heidi • 16. Romeo y Julieta
17. Los buscadores de tesoros • 19. La hija del capitán
20. Pollyanna • 21. Capitanes intrépidos • 22. Máquinas
23. Miguel Strogoff • 24. La vida en los castillos

Nivel 4. El placer de *LEER*

1. Los viajes de Gulliver • 2. Drácula • 3. Robinson Crusoe
4. De la Tierra a la Luna • 5. Viaje al centro de la Tierra
6. Frankenstein • 7. Veinte mil leguas de viaje submarino
8. Cinco semanas en globo • 9. Ben-Hur
10. Aventuras de Sherlock Holmes • 11. Oliver Twist
12. David Copperfield • 13. Las minas del rey Salomón • 14. Jane Eyre
15. Cuentos de la Alhambra • 16. Corazón • 17. Leyendas de Bécquer
18. Colmillo Blanco • 19. Los domadores de dragones
20. Aventuras de piratas • 21. Don Quijote de la Mancha
22. Dos años de vacaciones • 23. Lawrence de Arabia
24. El diario de Ana Frank • 25. Cuentos de terror • 26. Ivanhoe
27. La Primera Guerra Mundial